LOVE'S REFRACTION

Jealousy and Compersion in Queer Women's Polyamorous Relationships

Popular wisdom might suggest that jealousy is an inevitable outcome of non-monogamous relationships. In *Love's Refraction*, Jillian Deri explores the distinctive question of how and why polyamorists – people who practise consensual non-monogamy – manage jealousy. Her focus is on the polyamorist concept of "compersion" – taking pleasure in a lover's other romantic and sexual encounters.

By discussing the experiences of queer, lesbian, and bisexual polyamorous women, Deri highlights the social and structural context that surrounds jealousy. Her analysis, making use of the sociology of emotion and feminist intersectionality theory, shows how polyamory challenges traditional emotional and sexual norms.

Clear and concise, *Love's Refraction* speaks to both the academic and the polyamorous community. Deri lets her interviewees speak for themselves, linking academic theory and personal experiences in a sophisticated, engaging, and accessible way.

JILLIAN DERI received her PhD in Sociology from Simon Fraser University.

T0350045

Love's Refraction

Jealousy and Compersion in Queer Women's Polyamorous Relationships

JILLIAN DERI

UNIVERSITY OF TORONTO PRESS
Toronto Buffalo London

© University of Toronto Press 2015
Toronto Buffalo London
www.utppublishing.com

ISBN 978-1-4426-3709-2 (cloth)
ISBN 978-1-4426-2869-4 (paper)

Library and Archives Canada Cataloguing in Publication

Deri, Jillian, 1976–, author
Love's refraction : jealousy and compersion in queer women's polyamorous
relationships / Jillian Deri.

Includes bibliographical references and index.
ISBN 978-1-4426-3709-2 (bound). – ISBN 978-1-4426-2869-4 (pbk.)

1. Non-monogamous relationships. 2. Lesbians. 3. Jealousy. 4. Love –
Psychological aspects. I. Title.

HQ980.D47 2015   306.84′23086643   C2014-907922-2

This book has been published with the help of a grant from the Federation for the
Humanities and Social Sciences, through the Awards to Scholarly Publications
Program, using funds provided by the Social Sciences and Humanities Research
Council of Canada.

University of Toronto Press acknowledges the financial assistance to its publishing
program of the Canada Council for the Arts and the Ontario Arts Council, an agency
of the Government of Ontario.

Canada Council   Conseil des Arts
for the Arts   du Canada

ONTARIO ARTS COUNCIL
CONSEIL DES ARTS DE L'ONTARIO
an Ontario government agency
un organisme du gouvernement de l'Ontario

University of Toronto Press acknowledges the financial support of the Government
of Canada through the Canada Book Fund for its publishing activities.

Contents

Acknowledgments

For my parents, Eva and Tom: After cradling me in your unconditional love, you have inspired me to foster that depth of love in all my relationships. Mom, I continue to feel your love and it is the source of endless joy. Köszönöm, és imadlok.

Mike Robertson: Thank you for the joy, the laughter, and the beauty.

Catherine Deri-Armstrong: Thank you for both challenging and encouraging me every step of the way.

Tamara Unroe: I jump off this cliff with you as my Wingsuit.

Kira Schaffer: You inspire my patience and teach me the joy of inversion, dangling, and slowing down.

Gabriela Rosales: Thank you for always believing in me and in the power of fashion.

A.J. Murray: Thank you for making polyamory beautiful in my life.

Megan Amaral: Thank you for melding critical thinking with creative play. The world needs social connectors and community builders like you.

Meta and Veronica: Thank you for demonstrating the depth of compersion's beauty.

My study participants and the poly community: Thank you for your continued inspiration, the necessary complexity, and your immense support.

Doug Hildebrand and my anonymous peer reviewers: Your support and challenges brought this text to the next level. I have so much gratitude for your effort, encouragement, and attention to detail.

Special thanks to Ann Travers, Michael Hathaway, Mary Bryson, Helen Leung, Great Northern Way Aerial Club, Mitch and Camp

Beaverton, Luke and Jana, Philippe and Camp Friends and Lovers, Vivienne, Milena, Mary, Sean, Becca, Targol, Bryan, Nici and Mike, Jennifer, Sandra, Teresa, Jenn, Phresha, Little Woo, Stephanie, Kari, Kat, Fayza, Wendy, Bethany, Ron, Naomi and Luciterra, James, Trevor, Mel, Dayna, Alycia, Sage, Etai, and Burning Man. Oodles of gratitude for all the theorists, authors, and brilliant minds who continually inspire me.

LOVE'S REFRACTION

Jealousy and Compersion in Queer Women's
Polyamorous Relationships

1 But Don't You Get Jealous?

When I am discussing polyamory, the two most common responses I receive are "I could never do that; I would get too jealous" and "where do you find the time?" Although the time question remains a mystery, I find the issue of jealousy absolutely fascinating. The assumptions implied in this remark sparked my research into how polyamorists are affected by jealousy. Popular wisdom suggests that non-monogamy is impossible; if one's lover has sexual encounters outside the relationship, jealousy will be the inevitable and intolerable outcome. At the same time, jealousy is viewed as a sign of love, and thus the expected and appropriate reaction to a partner's sexual or romantic activities or interests outside of the relationship. By this logic, we would expect polyamory to be the cause of jealousy and monogamy to be the cure. Yet there is no shortage of stories of jealousy in otherwise monogamous relationships. By engaging in multiple relationships, polyamorists do exactly what conventional knowledge deems dangerous and unsavoury. Polyamorous people may indeed experience jealousy, but the circumstances are different, and consequently the experience and embodiment of jealousy is also different from dominant portrayals of jealousy. This book explores this question: how, and why, do polyamorists manage jealousy?

Non-monogamy has existed throughout most of recorded human history (Clanton and Smith 1977; Mead 1968; Ryan and Jetha 2010). Contemporary Western culture, however, privileges monogamy as a natural and superior form of family and relationship organization (Ryan and Jetha 2010). Within the last few decades, polyamory has emerged as a "burgeoning sexual story" (Barker 2005), with its own discourse and cultural practice. Polyamory is commonly defined as a form of non-monogamy where people maintain multiple, simultaneous sexual and emotional relationships and where all parties are aware and consenting (Sheff 2005; Haritaworn, Lin, and Klesse 2006). The word "polyamory" is used in a variety of ways to describe a sexual identity, sexual preference, discourse, politic, practice, and philosophy, or as Robinson (2013, 21) argues, a "strategy of sexual expression." Polyamory (often called "poly" by its practitioners) differs from swinging in its emphasis on emotional intimacy and longer-term commitments. Polyamory differs from polygamy (wherein a husband can have several wives) in its emphasis on gender equality; in polyamory both men and women are free to have multiple partners. Polyamory differs from adultery in its focus on honesty, consent, and full disclosure by all parties involved (Sheff 2005). In practice, however, there is significant overlap among the identities, practices, communities, and discourses of these categories. Also, there is a vast range in how people who espouse polyamory do and do not abide by these criteria. Unlike many sexual identities that were named top-down by scientific "experts," the term "polyamory" emerged from within the community itself, and poly-amorists have worked to have the term recognized as a legitimate sexual identity category (such as by the Kinsey Institute).[1]

Plummer (2001) developed the concept of emotion world to describe the ways in which a culture's words and concepts shape people's emotional responses. Polyamorist theory critiques the "dominant assumptions of the normalcy and naturalness of monogamy" (Barker and Langdridge 2010b, 750) – dubbed compulsory monogamy or mononormativity (Ritchie and Barker 2006) – as well as its norms regarding emotion, sexuality, and heterosexuality and thus how it shapes people's view of relationships (Sheff 2006). In much of Western culture, for example, the idea of sexual exclusivity is part of our emotion world; it is held up as the epitome of love and commitment, and hence any digression from this path is constructed as if it should be met with distrust and jealousy. Polyamorists try to re-craft their approach to love, relationships, sexuality, and emotions in ways that minimize instances of jealousy. They strive for jealousy to be superseded by compersion, a term used by polyamorous people to describe feelings of pleasure in response to a lover's romantic or sexual encounters outside the relationship.

---

1   http://www.kinseyinstitute.org/.

One aspect of this emotion world is its feeling rules, a concept Hoch-schild (1979) developed to refer to the cultural norms that dictate how one is supposed to feel in a given situation. Relatedly, there are also dis-play rules that tell us how and when emotions ought to be expressed. Even though feeling and display rules tend to be unwritten, we often notice them when we break a norm, such as the social response to some-one laughing at a funeral or cheerfully breaking up with a lover. The polyamorist community questions the feeling rules associated with monogamy, romantic love, and jealousy and has developed alternate feeling rules, creating norms and strategies that steer their practice as a subculture, as opposed to each individual negotiating jealousy in iso-lation. These rules include ways to initiate communication, negotiate boundaries, and structure disclosure. In doing so, polyamorists attempt to create a lifestyle where jealousy is neither inevitable nor intolerable and where the emotional experience of compersion is not only possible but actually common. Thus, this book asks, what are these polyamorous feeling rules? In what way do these rules inform polyamorists' experi-ence of jealousy? How and to what extent do polyamorists resist the regulation of emotion and sexuality and create alternatives that better meet their needs? To what extent do these re-imagined emotion worlds translate into instances of compersion, or to what extent do they merely reproduce the dominant model that they are attempting to re-envision? Thus, instead of focusing on the individual as the locus of emotional-ity, my book enquires into the co-constitutive connection between the self and the social in the (re)construction, experience, and expression of emotions.

For my research, I spoke with polyamorous queer, lesbian, and bisex-ual women in Vancouver, Canada, about how and why they practise polyamory and how they experience, manage, and re-imagine jealousy within open relationships. I sought to understand additional questions. What stories of jealousy emerge from the culture and experience of polyamorous queer women in Vancouver? How does a re-imagining of love and jealousy shift embodied affect? What challenges, contradic-tions, and tensions exist within polyamorous culture? Is the experience of polyamory enough to overcome polyagony?

"Polyagony" is a tongue-in-cheek polyamorous term that serves as a reminder that jealousy can sometimes be excruciating. Jealousy is not the only permutation of polyagony, but it is a predominant source of angst to many polyamorists. My interest in this uncomfortable feel-ing stems in part from the soft taboo surrounding jealousy. Although jealousy is expected in dominant culture, it is often accompanied by embarrassment. As a result, people tend to downplay their jealousy and recast their behaviour as a matter of honour, pride, or anger (Clanton 1996). People tend to dislike experiencing jealousy yet sometimes take pride when they elicit this emotion in others. Jealousy occurs at the intersection of contradictory feelings: love and hate, romance and heartbreak, excitement and fear. On its lighter side, jealousy has been linked to difficult feelings, emotional immaturity, overdependence, and possessiveness (Baumgart 1990; Clanton and Smith 1977; White and Mullen 1989; Salovey 1991). On its graver side, jealousy is associated with controlling relationships, aggression, or misogynist violence (Ben-Ze'ev and Goussinsky 2008; Edalati and Redzuan 2010; Klesse 2006b; Speed and Ganstead 1997; Yates 2000). It cannot be understated that jealousy is also a common reprehensible justification for abusive behaviour and domestic violence.[2]

As Ngai (2005) makes clear, an analysis of these "ugly feelings," so named for their unpleasantness, reveals a great deal about the structures and institutions from which they emerge. Jealousy may be experienced as an internal feeling, but it is embedded in a larger social context, evidenced by the fact that the causes of jealousy and how it is expressed vary significantly cross-culturally and temporally, as well as by gender, age, and class (Clanton and Smith 1977; Mead 1968; Stearns 1989; Hart and Legerstee 2010). The study of jealousy is important in understanding the emotional experience of polyamorists because it is often cited as a barrier to successful polyamory (Easton and Liszt 1997; Labriola 2013; Taormino 2008). For polyamorists, mitigating jealousy is often considered a site for critical resistance, with compersion (or at least a lack of jealousy) the ultimate goal.

Methodology

For my research, I used qualitative, semi-structured, open-ended interviews to speak with 22 self-identified polyamorous queer, lesbian, and bisexual women in Vancouver, Canada, recruited through posts in online polyamorous communities and word of mouth. Because my research is primarily centred on a social movement and cultural practice, my research is informed by both academic and popular literature.

---

2   Notably, my research does not address aggressive or violent expressions of jealousy.

I intentionally do not manufacture a dichotomy or a hierarchy between these bodies of knowledge, grounding such an inclination in my feminist intersectionality perspective. Because polyamorous blogs, journalistic advice columns, popular non-fiction, and self-help books, for example, may inspire significant sway over a polyamorist's theory and practice, these works inform my analysis. This does not mean that all information is equally valid, but rather that sociological rigour can be applied to multiple and innovative sources of information, particularly when it comes to analysis of a sexual and emotional practice. Feminist intersectionality emphasizes the importance of integrating material that remains relevant to the researched community and those to whom the information will be disseminated. With a feminist intersectional approach, I intentionally decline any jargon and deliberately retain accessible language through an approachable grounding of theory. Conventional disciplinary boundaries are shifting as new information technology has significantly modified the availability and hierarchy of information – in other words, people who work outside of academia are equally contributing to the dialogue that informs polyamory discourse. Indeed, the Internet is an information leveller. I hope my readers will find my intersectional approach to sources and discourses refreshing.

Following feminist intersectionality's emphasis on transparency, I will locate myself within this research: I am a queer bisexual woman who has practised both polyamory and monogamy, and I reside in Vancouver, BC. I am actively engaged with the queer and polyamorous communities, both in Vancouver and online. Thus, I approach the topic as an insider to polyamorous practice. As someone with a critical yet pro-polyamory position, I assume polyamorous queer women have insight into the sociology of jealousy, but I initially approached my research with an open curiosity as to what this may be. While I fully acknowledge the role of people's psychological disposition in the experience of emotions, my focus for this project is the role of socio-culture. Notably, the sociological and the psychological are far from mutually exclusive. Indeed, the validity of their co-formation is increasingly verified (Lehrer 2009). It is my hope that a follow-up study engages with the experience of polyamorous jealousy through a critical psychological lens.

After reviewing the research on jealousy of the last 50 years (with a few key earlier thinkers), I found that emotions are often understood in relation to popular metaphors or the predominant technologies of the time. Contemporary portrayals of emotion often use the Internet as a metaphor in that they describe emotions as a complex web of interconnections that are in constant flux. It is no surprise that one of the key lexicons of contemporary feminist and embodiment scholarship is intersectionality. Emotion, in much contemporary research, is portrayed as developing interdependently with and perpetually interacting with reason. Emotion emerges from the biosocial feedback between the body and culture, the individual and the collective. In most research, emotion is still gendered with the assumption of a two-gender system, but the range of emotional diversity portrayed by each gender is now recognized to be more complicated. In particular, in line with intersectionality, as well as the affective turn in social research (Clough and Halley 2007), I theorize from a position that integrates multiple perspectives, complicates mutually exclusive divides, and substantiates accounts from opposing perspectives. My research into polyamorous queer women offers insight into a feminist approach to emotions.

My aim is to maintain a non-judgmental approach to the sexual practices of polyamory and its attending emotions and thus to analyse jealousy's manifestation without imposing my ideas of "bad" or of "ought." At the same time, I do not wish to treat jealousy as benign, since it can be a challenging emotion. I evaluate the stigma and shame attached to jealousy, while recognizing jealousy as a barrier to intimacy and as a limiting factor in polyamorous relationships. To many people, jealousy does not feel good, but it does play an important and potentially revealing role. The culture of polyamory creates the potential for a non-judgmental approach to jealousy by developing creative emotional practices to alleviate unpleasant experiences. As I once heard in a workshop on polyamory: "don't should all over yourself." In other words, critical and constructive analysis of challenging emotional experiences can be developed without relying on conventional judgments and hierarchies.

Summary of Participants

From my initial inquiry, I had an inclination that the queer women's polyamorous population would demonstrate unique cultural features. By inquiring into a smaller subset of the polyamorous community, I sought to investigate how shared cultural discourse might influence the emotional embodiment of jealousy and compersion. The literature on jealousy demonstrates particularly gendered scripts, and I was curious about how such gendered feeling rules might be queered. I hypothesized that unique values, troubles, and power dynamics would emerge from this population, which also happens to be especially under-studied.

Of my 22-person sample, 15 identify as queer, 3 as lesbian, and 4 as bisexual. They range in age from 25 to 62. The median age of my participants is 37, and the mean is 38.5. Although the majority of participants identify as white, other ethnicities and identities include mixed-race, Asian Canadian, Australian Canadian, and First Nations. Of those who identified their religion/spirituality, the following are represented: Jewish, Pagan, Wiccan, Buddhist, Christian/Catholic, and atheist. Participants' specific occupations are omitted to protect their identity, but my sample includes the following categories of careers: physical labourer, academic, student, administrator, clinical counsellor, manager, sex worker, social worker, web designer, stay-at-home parent, artist, retail worker, and health care practitioner. Socio-economic backgrounds range from working class to middle class. Seven of my participants are parents. Three were born outside of Canada. All lived in the Greater Vancouver region at the time of my study. All speak English as their primary language. All names used in this book are pseudonyms, and all identifying features have been modified to maintain their anonymity.

The women in my sample participated in a wide range of relationship structures, including triads, primary relationships with sex on the side, long-term monogamy, marriage, singledom, cohabitation with one primary, cohabitation with two lovers (who are not lovers with each other), cohabitation with three lovers (who are lovers with each other), cohabitation with a family of past and current lovers, having a primary and a secondary lover, and having two primaries. The longest polyamorous relationship reported by my participants was going on 11 years at the time of my interview, and the second longest had reached 9.5 years. Three of my participants identified as genderqueer, all of whom were comfortable participating in my study and being categorized as women as a result of their partial or historical identification as queer women. The vast majority of the sample identified as feminists, although they differed widely in their definitions of feminism (which will be discussed in detail in chapter 4). Only one participant mentioned being polyamorous with regular participation in the swinging community. Close to two-thirds of the participants identified as kinky or interested in BDSM (bondage, discipline, sadism, and masochism) practices.

A couple of my participants became polyamorous unintentionally in that they happened to fall in love with two people at the same time and the situation played out in such a manner that acting on this desire was permissible. For example, Martha stated,

> At the time I went to therapy and was like, there is something wrong with me. I'm in love with two people and they are both women and I'm really fucked up about it... ... Then the therapist had given me this book, *The Ethical Slut*, and I'm like oh my gosh, there is a whole book written about this, because I thought I was very abnormal because I had all this psych training that would suggest I was abnormal.

A few participants claimed to be "wired" to simultaneously love more than one person romantically, while still others stated that they grew to prefer polyamory through exposure to polyamorous ideas by their peers. Other participants were exposed to polyamory by a person they were dating or interested in dating. Two of my participants came to polyamory through an idea suggested in a written text, offering evidence for "erotic plasticity," the degree to which culture or social factors can influence one's sexual desires (Baumeister 2000).

Although my research focused on a small group of individuals, the insights into the restructuring of emotion worlds resonates with the wider communities of polyamorists interconnected online. The research reveals the influence of the social ideas of monogamy, commitment, and polyamory, which have implications for multiple kinds of relationship structures. After all, Haritaworn, Lin, and Klesse (2006, 518) contend that

> an engagement with polyamory and non-monogamy can provide novel insights into the social construction and organization of kinship, households and the family, parenting practices, sexual identities and heteronormativity. What is more, polyamory opens up new sex-positive terrains for erotic, sexual and relational understandings and practices.

A Short Note on Love

A study of polyamory or jealousy is also a study of love. Love has been traversed in depth by musicians, artists, poets, literary scholars, spiritual teachers, clinical counsellors, and psychologists, yet historically the sociological focus on love has been marginalized (Brown 2006; Jackson 1993). Sociological methodology is troubled by love because of its immeasurability, its relativity, its variegated definitions and the general dismissal of matters of the heart in most "serious" studies. The word "love" has countless applications: it is used to describe how we feel about chocolate, movies, and dogs as well as the connection between soulmates. Still, using the word "love" can render an academic a vague, naive sentimentalist, calling into question the credibility of one's research.

Yet, as Jackson (1993) cleverly points out, "even sociologists fall in love." Far from frivolity, love, compassion, and connectivity contribute to what drives our social world. Even Freud believed that "psychoanalysis is in essence a cure through love."[3] I suspect that the de-legitimization of love as an area of sociological research points less to the immeasurability of love than to the hierarchical split between emotion and reason. Love can be a risky topic for a scholar to pursue, even though an understanding of love and its construction, effect, and circulation is important for understanding social dynamics, creativity, art, politics, and even economics.

Even if love's permutations are particularly varied, love is arguably a universal human phenomenon.[4] At the same time, love is also an emotional experience heavily laden with ideology and gendered feeling rules. Indeed, romantic love is a relatively new requirement for marriage, which has historically been based on economic and political arrangements. Ben-Ze'ev and Goussinsky (2008, xi–xii) argue that the ideology of romantic love includes the belief that

> the beloved is everything to the lover and hence love is all you need; true love lasts forever and can conquer all; true lovers are united – they are one and the same person; love is irreplaceable and exclusive; and love is pure and can do no evil.

True love, they argue, is idealized as eternal and self-sacrificial and has "unlimited justification" (ibid., xii). They argue that since these beliefs are idealized, they are far from realistic, and the disjuncture between the ideology and its attainability can lead to dangerous situations. In particular they cite statistics on violence inspired by jealousy and other "horrific crimes in the name of the altruistic ideas of religion and love" (ibid., xii).

---

3 Freud, in a letter to Jung, cited in Brown (2000, 39).

4 While I recognize the dangers of ever assigning a single trait to be universal to humankind, I am taking the risk of entrusting love to this claim. People may ascribe an array of emotions and subjects to love, including parental, familial, friendship, and companion species, yet as social creatures, we tend to form affectionate bonds with others that are akin to love.

According to Brown (2000, 44), "the romantic narrative survives despite its deconstruction in the social sciences … precisely because it speaks to the biological fact that we are object seeking from birth, a state of which the romantic narrative could be seen to be a psychological elaboration." She turns to Melanie Klein's (1997) object relations theory for an explanation of our biological urge to connect with an object (i.e., a person who holds our affectionate interest), formed and modelled by our earliest attachment to our mothers, as it is reproduced in adult romantic relationships.

Historical and contemporary courtship is guided by socialized gendered feeling rules of love. Indeed, a significant portion of claims to masculinity and femininity are exhibited through displays of love and sexuality. There are gendered conventions regarding romantic gestures, emotional attachments, pursuits, chivalry, and most demonstrations of affection. Examples of breached gendered feeling rules would be a soft, romantic man or either an aggressive woman or an emotionally distant woman. A person's partner is often thought to be a reflection of their gender. Take the archetypical example of the captain of the football team and his cheerleading girlfriend, where one's girl/boyfriend represents a successful manifestation of gender. Or consider the stereotype of a man and his "trophy wife," where the other is sought out as a wish-fulfilment of successful gender, be it financial or aesthetic.

Clearly, there is a gendered dance to love. And yet these gendered roles are being transformed as gender relations change. Giddens (1992, 85) argues that the contemporary "transformation of intimacy" is a movement away from romantic narrative towards the pure relationship, revering instead intimacy and gender equality. Instead of being based on vows, the pure relationship is based on trust, and it is

> entered into for its own sake, for what can be derived by each person from a sustained association with another and which is continued only in so far as it is thought by both parties to deliver enough satisfaction for each individual to stay within it.

This is, indeed, an idealized structure for polyamorists.

The question is thus, by what components of romantic love do polyamorists abide and which do they critique or rewrite? Can romantic love be understood apart from our socially constructed romantic narrative?

While the term "polyamory" emphasizes the centrality of love to its practice (i.e., many loves), love cannot simply be conflated with polyamorous practice. Many polyamorous practices contain degrees of non-monogamies – that is, sexual explorations outside one's relationship rather than primarily emotional connections. Also, love is not necessarily conditional to emotional connections. What does differentiate polyamory from other forms of non-monogamy, however, is its primacy of potential emotional affections for all parties involved as well as at least a friendship level of respect between all those engaged in the relationship (i.e., lover's lovers). Also, the focus on emotionality over sexuality should not suggest that sexuality is undervalued. Doubtless, sexuality is one of the distinguishing features indicating that these relationships are not solely friendship.

Polyamorist culture eschews the sexually and emotionally exclusive focus of romantic ideology and yet maintains the importance of love. Whereas dominant culture might agree with St Augustine, who said, "He that is not jealous is not in love," polyamorists are generally critical of the idea that a partner's jealousy represents their love and commitment to the relationship. Polyamorists rework some common romantic complaints, while they also take some romantic notions even further than a monogamist might. For example, polyamorists tend to be sceptical of the idea that true romance is everlasting and is necessarily accompanied by a lack of attraction to other people. Polyamory also challenges the idea that one's romantic partner should be able to fulfil all of one's needs or that a partner should be endlessly devoted to one person. On the other hand, polyamorists preserve the importance of love and romantic connections, as well as the significance of emotional affection in sexual encounters. After all, polyamorists make more romantic commitments, not fewer. Polyamorous ideals and critiques of love are described throughout this book, along with their views on jealousy and compersion.

Chapter Overview

In the following chapter, "Polyagony: An Exploration of Jealousy," I describe how jealousy tends to be understood within the parameters of a monogamous model, which contributes to the way it is experienced and expressed. For example, in a language that does not have a word for the opposite of jealousy, there is an implication that compersion does not exist. Thus, I compare this body of research with polyamorous ideas of jealousy and compersion. Grounded in feminist intersectionality theory and the sociology of emotion, I introduce my approach to jealousy as an intersectional emotion. Next, I highlight several key terms in the polyamorous lexicon in order to familiarize the reader with the culture of polyamory. Because polyamory emerged in part from a critique of mono-normativity, I describe misconceptions of monogamy's role in the maintenance of social well-being.

In chapter 3, "If You Move to the Rainforest, You've Got No Right to Complain about the Rain: From Polyagony to Compersion," I describe some of my findings on how polyamorists experience, express, and navigate their jealousy. My research reveals the prevalence of tensions and contradictions within the subculture's approach to difficult emotions associated with open relationships. I found that instead of each individual working through their personal emotional trials, polyamorists build a culture around polyamory, with particular norms and etiquette developed in part with the intention of enabling the experience of compersion. However, as with most etiquette, the rules are not always followed, they are always in flux, and the norms in place to mitigate jealousy do not work for everybody. Within my sample, jealousy is described as a difficult and challenging emotion but one that is tolerable and manageable. In this chapter, I also address some of the other challenges of polyamory that arose within the research, including time pressures, issues regarding parenting, and maintaining safer sex practices. To balance my descriptions of polyagony, I conclude the chapter with a discussion of the rewards and benefits resulting from polyamorists' practice.

In chapter 4, "Once You Say 'I'm Poly,' It Kind of Eliminates the Need for the Feminist Part: Gender, Jealousy, and Polyamory," I analyse jealousy within polyamory in terms of gender, feminism, and queerness. My research reveals that the gender divide is more complicated than certain research and representations of jealousy suggest. I investigate how my participants re-imagine and recreate the gendered feeling rules of jealousy and the extent to which they are successful in such a re-imagining. Polyamorous communities are portrayed in the literature as strongly pro-feminist, and while my sample reflects this political leaning, there is much variation in how feminism is defined and demonstrated, particularly with regard to reclamation of promiscuity, competition between women, and emotional control.

In chapter 5, "Jealousy Can Be Hot if You Flip It: Working and Playing with Power," I investigate the intersection of polyamory, jealousy, and power relations. Jealousy within polyamory is inextricably linked to power on two levels: through interpersonal relationships and through the regulation of sexuality and emotion. Although the definition of power is relative and individual, this chapter addresses how power is perceived and operates within relationships in terms of practical matters (such as investment in the relationship, financial power, quantity of lovers, etc.) and reconstructions of power (playful jealousy and sexual practice). I look at how the regulation of sexuality and the subsequent marginalization of polyamory affect my participants, as well as their resistance to such power structures. My participants found creative ways to interpret, construct, and re-imagine power relations. At times, they found ways to mitigate negative emotions associated with power imbalance without necessarily diminishing the inequity itself. In other instances, however, power re-emerged in conventional hierarchical patterns. Polyamorists' re-imaginings of emotional power both within their relationships and in relation to the larger social framework offer insight into the social context of jealousy.

In my concluding remarks, "Polyamory's Legacy," I highlight the central themes that emerge within this book. Questions about polyamory are often concerned with the viability of compersively loving multiple people, and this concern reflects cultural notions of love. While considering instances of both compersion and polygony, I focus on polyamorist culture and resistance to mono-normativity. Although polyamory is likely to remain a minority practice, the cultural values of polyamory have the potential to challenge contemporary culture's treatment of jealousy, feeling rules, gender, and the regulation of emotion and sexuality.

2 Polyagony: An Exploration of Jealousy

As a jealous person, I suffer fourfold: because I am jealous, because I reproach myself for my jealousy, because I fear that my jealousy is hurting the other, because I allow myself to be enslaved by a banality: I suffer from being excluded, from being aggressive, from being crazy, and from being common.

Roland Barthes

The jealous are possessed by a mad devil and a dull spirit at the same time.

Johann Kaspar Lawater

Jealousy as an Intersectional Emotion

Jealousy, that dragon which slays love under the pretense of keeping it alive.

Havelock Ellis

People use the word "jealousy" to refer to a wide variety of sensations: from small twinges of discomfort to overwhelming rages, which are different not only in degree but also in kind. Some people use the word "jealousy" when they do not feel it deeply (I'm so jealous of your new shoes) and deny it when the emotion is likely to be strong (I don't care at all if he is dating her now). The use of the term "jealousy" varies both in academia and in popular discourse. People differ in their description of how jealousy feels, the events that cause it, and the behaviours associated with it. Guerrero, Trost, and Yoshimura (2005, 233) define romantic jealousy as

> a multi-faceted set of affective, behavioral, and cognitive responses that occur when the existence and/or quality of a person's primary relationship is threatened by a third party.

Although this definition makes reference to primary relationships, any relationship can be subject to jealousy. My study looks at how people manage jealousy in relationships where the inclusion of a "third party" is openly negotiated and thus their exclusion is not the preferred strategy to mitigate jealousy. Jealousy is a complex experience that combines many emotions, including fear, anger, sadness, betrayal, pride, loss, and grief, and it is for this reason that some theorists are reluctant to call it a distinct emotion on its own (Hart and Legerstee 2010; Hupka and Ryan 1990). Hence, for many theorists jealousy refers to the emotion, feeling, state, character trait, or "emotional episode" of a situation, a multitude of feelings related to the situation, actions, and often a resolution (Parrott 1991, 4). It is important to note that both real and imagined threats can incite jealousy, which is why an illusory scenario can trigger an emotional reaction.

It is useful to distinguish between two types of jealousy: suspicious and fait accompli jealousy (Parrott 1991). Suspicious jealousy is the feeling of distrust or doubt in relation to a partner's faithfulness or commitment to the relationship. An example would be an intuition that a lover was breaking an agreed-upon rule or a sense that they are pulling away their affection. In contrast, fait accompli jealousy is where the threat or "rival" is known or the relationship is in real jeopardy, such as when a lover has left one person for another. Jealousy is closely related to envy, which can also be subdivided into two groups: malicious versus non-malicious envy (Parrott 1991). Non-malicious envy is the feeling of wanting something that someone else has (such as a relationship with a certain person). Coveting is a form of non-malicious envy but implies a wrongful desire for the object/subject. Malicious envy is the feeling or impulse of wanting someone not to have the object/subject that you desire, wanting this object destroyed, or spitefully wanting bad things to happen to this person. For example, someone does not want to get back together with an ex-lover but still does not (yet) wish her happiness in her new relationship (which is an experience that many people find too shameful to admit). A common manifestation of malicious envy is to spread spiteful gossip or display cattiness about an ex-lover's new partner or a more successful co-worker (see Barash 2006). Malicious envy is the flip side of the German term "schadenfreude," the feeling of taking pleasure in another person's misfortune. Fait accompli jealousy frequently accompanies malicious envy, where a person wishes bad fortune upon their romantic rival. This might explain why some people's jealous anger is directed towards their rival rather than towards their own lover (Yates 2007).

Simmel (1955) notes that jealousy and envy require a feeling of entitlement regarding the possession of an object/subject. Thus, people are more likely to experience jealousy or envy concerning people in their lives than in relation to a celebrity, for example. Similarly, Yates (2007, 25) argues that sometimes envy is about possession for possession's sake as opposed to actually wanting the object/subject. Simmel (1955, 51) also includes a third distinction within the family of envy and jealousy: begrudging, which he defines as

> the envious desire of an object, not because it is especially desirable but because the other has it [and it is] accompanied by the utter unbearability of the thought that the other possesses it.

Jealousy, as with all emotions, is manifested in/on the body, with physical and psychological symptoms. At the same time, culture plays a role in how jealousy is experienced, how one appraises the situation in which it arises, and how jealousy is expressed. Jealousy is a social emotion in that it is experienced in relation to another person (real or imagined). Also, jealousy requires a scenario or context (real or imagined). Lazarus (1991, 284) wrote, "Hope cannot be distinguished from what is hoped for any more than anger can be divorced from what one is angry about." Similarly, Parkinson states, "we don't just feel angry, for example, we feel angry with someone else, about something they have done" (Parkinson, Fischer, and Manstead 2005, 10). Consequently, I ground my theory in work that highlights the intersection of sociological, cultural, psychological, and biological processes in the formation, experience, and expression of emotion (Hart and Legerstee 2010; Williams and Bendelow 1996). Sara Ahmed (2004b, 27) argues,

> Rather than seeing emotions as psychological dispositions, we need to consider how they work, in concrete and particular ways, to mediate the relationship between the psychic and the social, and between the individual and collective.

In addition, Harding and Pribram (2004, 865) contend that even though emotions tend to be understood as individual and private affairs,

> emotions are formed and function as part of the historical, cultural, and political contexts in which they are practiced to reproduce, and potentially resist, hegemonic relations.

I investigate how polyamorists' cultural and collective beliefs (not solely individual beliefs) translate into feeling, at times both enabling and preventing the experience of jealousy and compersion. Further, these collective feelings are transformed into "an act of reading and recognition" (Ahmed 2004a, 29), so that internalized cultural practices and embodied ideas reveal themselves narratively. In other words, I examine how polyamorists' affective experiences of jealousy are understood and re-imagined through their narratives and verbalized understanding. Through my research, the emotion of jealousy is revealed to be at once a function of social ideas about love, monogamy, and polyamory and experienced as a bodily sensation that is interpreted and resisted through conscious understanding of those feelings.

Emotions are rarely experienced as singular feelings. Jealousy tends to be mixed with other feelings including affection, love, fondness, sadness, pride, bitterness, anger, etc. (each person has a personalized set of associated emotions). Beyond that, the boundary of what qualifies as "jealousy" is also ambiguous. Although most people experience jealousy in a multitude of ways, the term "jealousy" is still useful because it frames the discussion and moves away from free-floating emotionality, which is also not accurate. Saying "I feel jealous" will elicit nods of understanding rather than utter confusion. Yet the limits of the emotional experience of jealousy are rarely clear-cut. I have experienced both fierce sensations and fleeting twinges, both of which I am apt to label jealousy, even if the actual sensations are highly varied. The kind of jealousy experienced also depends in part on one's disposition, affection, and sense of entitlement. People rarely experience jealousy related to someone with whom they feel no sense of attachment, care, or similarity. That is why I call jealousy the shadow of love.

Although one potential outcome of a polyamorous practice is love's jealous shadow, another possible result is that of compersion; hence this book earned its title from another apt metaphor: love's refraction. Refractions are directional changes that result from the passage of matter through varying density. How might love morph when experienced through a polyamorous interface? While maintaining central properties, refraction can be a reflection of one's character, a modification of emotionality, or a change in modality. Although no metaphor captures all possibilities, I picture light refracting through a prism, highlighting multiple, and sometimes perceptional, outcomes of a journey.

I use the term "intersectional emotions" to highlight the intricate ways in which we convey constantly shifting feelings and to acknowledge the influence of feminist intersectionality on my work (see Hankivsky 2011). Feminist intersectionality theory owes a great debt to black feminist thought, in particular Patricia Hill Collins's (2000) matrix of oppression, wherein she expands an understanding of power beyond a single axis of either gender-, class-, or race-based subordination, thus integrating micro and macro levels of analysis within "interlocking systems of oppression." For example, not all queer people are subject to the same degree of marginalization since various social conditions contribute to one's experience. Racialization may exacerbate one's experience of homophobia while class privilege may minimize it. I utilize the term "intersectional emotions" to illustrate the complexity of factors which contribute to our experience of emotion, including biology, psychology, neurological composition, gender, age, culture, class, context, and other relevant factors. These factors are not solely additive, as in a combination of personal and cultural history, but rather multiply to produce an extensive range of embodied outcomes and power relations.

The body, the mind, and society are the sources and the sites of emotion, interacting in multiplicative ways. In other words, emotions are not solely the addition of body plus society. Rather, physiological, psychological (conscious and unconscious), and social dynamics interact to create unique and ever-changing outcomes, in multiple directions. Emotion and reason are not mutually exclusive, nor do they combine into one indistinguishable concept. Instead, emotion and reason continuously interact in any decision-making process or social experience, making them two sides of the same coin (see Lehrer 2009). Similarly, since we are enveloped with socialization from birth, one's cognitive process within a jealous episode, for example, is the shifting co-constitutive product of both nature and nurture.

Emotions are embodied manifestations of social practices and are subject to intersecting power relations. Such power relations operate at the level of individual, social, and systemic structures, and such power is always resisted, often creatively. With an intersectionality approach, I de-centre the idea of a unified, neutral subject and instead understand emotionality and power as dynamic processes. I emphasize the complexity and diversity of positionalities and approach social positioning as a process rather than a state. I aim for an account of polyamorous jealousy that evaluates emotion with emotion. With an intersectional approach, I also accept that because of the complex analysis, my understanding of emotionality and power relations can only ever be partial, a piece of the puzzle.

Comparing Monogamous and Polyamorous
Models of Jealousy

Often research on romantic jealousy assumes that the situation arose from a monogamous model of relationship, and hence also assumes that a third party is never welcome, rarely known, and necessarily a threat. Thus researchers often identify a partner's cheating or the suspicion of cheating as a "crisis event" from which to discuss jealousy (Bryson 1991, 202). The "rival" is the assumed archetype within jealousy-inducing circumstances. Ideally for polyamorists, having other lovers is consensual and pre-negotiated, and therefore the presence of another lover is not enough reason in itself for anyone to feel jealous. Polyamorists potentially experience jealousy under different circumstances then. The participants in my study reported feeling jealous when their partner started to date someone new, when the partner fell in love, when the other lover was too similar to themselves, when there were overlapping roles, when they felt less secure in their relationship, when they felt excluded, and quite often for no identifiable reason at all. Martha described sources of her and her partner's jealousy, based not necessarily on a rival but on a comparison to another known lover:

> When she sees me excited about other people, she feels a sense of fear and insecurity wondering if I will feel a deeper sense of connection with other people ... For me, it's fear ... A fear that somebody will be more interesting. A fear that my stress in my life is too much for her to handle and other people that she might encounter might feel easier to deal with. A fear that someone else will be better in bed. Fear of just not being good enough ... Fear that this person was more important than me.

Klarrisa described an instance of jealousy arising from a partner devoting particularly charged attention to another person:

> My primary partner is going on a date and she's all dressed up and can't remember the last time she got dressed up for me. And I'm jealous because she is full of new relationship energy and I feel neglected, abandoned, alone. And that happens all the time and that is not a new problem ... Sometimes I end up feeling like the old boot.

New relationship energy (NRE) is a term polyamorous people use to describe the early stages of romance, also known as infatuation, limerence, or the honeymoon period (Iantaffi 2010). The emotional surge at this time can interfere with one's affection towards others, and thus polyamorists take this into account when engaging in new relationships and try to act accordingly.

What polyamorists call "cheating" is lying or breaking an agreed-upon rule rather than having an outside sexual affair (Wosick-Correa 2010). Some polyamorists will avoid using the word "cheating" in order to avoid reifying mono-normative notions of infidelity (ibid.). The assumption in a monogamously oriented model is that a partner would experience jealousy if they suspected their partner was interested in or was seeing another person. A polyamorous person or one inclined towards non-monogamy could potentially be aware of this circumstance without jealousy being the outcome. This is not to say that polyamorists would never be jealous under these circumstances, but rather, their partner's interest in another person is not reason in itself to be jealous. Such an interest might even inspire compersion. If someone believes that true love is necessarily limited to one person, as is often standard in the monogamous model, they might retain a jealous fear of their partner leaving them for another monogamous relationship, but one who believes in polyamorous love might wish to include a third party into their relationship dynamic. In such a case, there might be fear of a decline in the quality of the relationship instead of the end of it.

The experience and expression of jealousy tends to be influenced also by socialization of gendered feeling rules. In his study of evolutionary psychology, for example, Buss (2000) argues that heterosexual men are inclined to respond with jealousy to a partner's (feared or real) sexual interactions with another, whereas heterosexual women tend to become jealous because of a partner's emotional attachment to another person. The discrepancy is explained by evolutionary developments of men's emphasis on paternity insecurity of a potential child, while women, as a result of a more significant physical investment, are concerned with the future emotional and material support of their mate. Buss also found that gay men find emotional unfaithfulness more challenging, yet there was no difference between heterosexual women and lesbians (ibid.). Carpenter (2012) discovered that for bisexuals, the gender of the partner in question influenced the discrepancy between sexual or emotional jealousy in ways not always consistent with the gender divide. Clanton (1996) found that men are socialized to deny jealousy, call it anger, and fight to avoid humiliation, and women are more likely to admit jealousy, internalize the blame, and work on the relationship.

Popular media representations of jealousy reinforce the stereotype that women express jealousy with cattiness, gossip, or manipulative behaviour, whereas men seem to express jealousy with anger, aggression, or violence.

Such generalizations, however, reveal more about cultural ideology and socialization than intrinsic truths about gender or jealousy. When a researcher begins with an assumption that men and women are two discrete entities, one will often find results to reinforce this assumption (Fausto-Sterling 2000; Fine 2010; Jordan-Young 2010). Such an assumption leads the enquirer to emphasize differences between genders rather than differences within a gender or similarities between genders, never mind questioning the construction of the dichotomy (Petersen 2004). Also, research tends to look for the causes of masculine and feminine traits as opposed to questioning what masculinity and femininity actually are (Jordan-Young 2010). Petersen (2004, 148) notes that researchers tend to assume monogamous heterosexuality is the norm and study the "other" as a deviation, which may influence "the conduct of research, and the interpretation and portrayal of findings." This has led to the assumption that monogamy is a "natural" or more civilized state of human behaviour, thus recording any deviations from sexual exclusivity as disproportionately negative, especially for women (Ryan and Jetha 2010).

Since Descartes, Western philosophy has been characterized by a theoretical dichotomy between reason and emotion, where reason is exalted and emotion is linked to irrationality, excess, and the feminine. Within this discourse, emotions are "antithetical to logical thinking and tend to be impulsive and intuitive" (Parkinson, Fischer, and Manstead 2005, 46). One of the problems with this perspective, according to Parkinson, is that it suggests that "emotions are involuntary, implying that the emotional individual is coerced into doing things that he or she has not really chosen to do" (ibid.). Indeed, there is a preoccupation with being in control. In more recent times, feminists and other theorists of emotion have challenged the legitimacy of this split and its subsequent hierarchy (Boler 1999; Grosz 1994; Jaggar 1989). Grosz (1994, 14) identifies the common assumption that "women are somehow more biological, more corporeal, and more natural than men." These feminists and sociologists of emotion challenge the idea that the only legitimate knowledge is knowledge based in reason; they instead recognize the value of emotional ways of knowing (Jaggar 1989). Even within this school of thought, however, jealousy may still be regarded as negative and weak, as a barrier to knowledge, and is often dismissed as paranoia or irrational insecurity. For many people, jealousy is too shameful to admit and is often described as crazy-making, erratic, or "taking over," which replicates the negative association of jealousy with out-of-control emotionality. Jealousy is also framed by our understanding of ownership (Robinson 1997) and thus control and entitlement over what is "ours."

Our understanding of that which is labelled emotional is culturally specific and requires an analysis of gender, race, class, and ability, since women, people of colour, the working class, and people with disabilities are disproportionally thought to be "overreacting" or "over the top" (Harding and Pribram 2002, 2004; Jaggar 1989; Parkinson, Fischer, and Manstead 2005), for which there are important consequences. Klesse (2006b, 647) argues,

> Jealousy is constructed in a way that justifies the control of women's bodies and sexuality and has the potential to legitimize all kinds of male violence and atrocities.

There is relatively more room for women to express emotion, whereas a man who is emotive may have his masculinity called into question (Jackson 1993). However, the degree to which women may express emotion is culturally circumscribed. Women who act on rather than verbalize certain emotions are seen as inappropriate. Crying may be seen as a feminine expression of an emotion, but too much crying is deemed "hysterical." "Normal" jealousy can be expressed in flirtatious jest, but excessive jealousy is seen as a sign of character weakness, low self-esteem, or even delusion or insanity (Clanton 2001).[5] Jealousy is further complicated by the way that some people take pleasure in knowing that someone is jealous of them and may even try to elicit this response in others.

The expression of jealousy is socially acceptable only within certain cultural and gender-specific parameters. Within a contemporary, Western, middle-class cultural framework for example, it is typically only acceptable to verbalize jealousy when there are identifiable reasons for its cause; rather than behaving jealously, one must speak calmly, such as saying, "I feel jealous with regard to you." When emotions are

---

5   Notably, my research does not address pathological, neurotic, or psychotic manifestations of jealousy, none of which were apparent in my sample population.

expressed this way, it is assumed that people are speaking their truth and are taking care of themselves by proactively asserting their needs (Zembylas and Fendler 2007). Other expressions of jealousy could be seen as "emotional" or "excessive."

Clanton's (2001) research reveals a shift in the cultural portrayal of jealousy in the American context. Prior to 1970, jealousy was often described as a "proof of love," coinciding with this period's emphasis on monogamy. Since the sexual revolution with its emphasis on personal freedom, choice, and control over one's body, jealousy is more often seen as the characteristic of a person who is "unduly possessive, insecure, and suffering from low self-esteem" (ibid., 160). Noting the shift in these perceptions, Clanton (1996, 173) argues that "jealousy is a socially-constructed emotion that changes to reflect changes in marriage rules, the adultery taboo, and gender roles." As polyamorous discourse reworks these same norms, does it have the potential to further shift our understanding of jealousy? It could be that as polyamorous discourse gains greater mainstream credibility, compersion may become more common. Not all polyamorous people are successful at alleviating jealousy, and at times they reinforce or repeat conventional manifestations of jealousy. But the discourse on polyamory challenges hegemonic structures of emotion by exposing the cultural ideology of jealousy while concurrently developing an alternative set of values, guidelines, and theories about it. Polyamorous people are not the only ones who experience compersion; they are, however, actively disseminating this concept and possible guidelines for its practice.

Jealousy is curiously stigmatized more than other difficult emotions. Rarely in Western culture is it shameful to express grief at the loss of a loved one. Indeed, it may be shameful when one does not express grief. And yet a culture that colludes in the construction of jealousy will still link the experience of jealousy to a sign of personal weakness. Furthermore, jealousy is not always a negative emotion. Jealousy can be used as a signifier of places of distress, can help one intuit a warning sign, and can even reinforce love, making it a useful emotional experience. There are also occasions when people exhibit a degree of emotional masochism and seem to take pleasure in the intensity of the experience that jealousy affords (as will be further discussed in chapter 5 in relation to playing with jealousy and its sexual transformations). With this emotional hypocrisy in mind, I attempt to discuss jealousy without any negative interpretation. While I recognize that most people do not enjoy the experience of jealousy, I attempt to complicate the simplistic divide that jealousy is negative and compersion is positive. I posit jealousy as a potentially difficult emotion but remove the judgment and shame that surround it.

Polyamory Terms

As the community has blossomed, polyamorists have developed vocabulary to describe their lifestyle and practices. What follows is a short index of the polyamorous lexicon.

Monogamy is the practice of having one sexual or romantic relationship for a given period of time, with emphasis on sexual exclusivity. There are subtle variations in the definition of monogamy: serial monogamy (consecutive relationships), social monogamy (people pairing up together to share resources, engage in sexual relations, raise children, or some combination) (Loue 2006, 4), sexual monogamy (sexual exclusivity), and emotional monogamy (highlights the intimacy component of one's affection or the person who is prioritized). The formal definition of monogamy implies marriage; however, the term "monogamy" is commonly applied to non-marital as well as marital relationships. Institutional monogamy refers to the way that monogamy is the only culturally and legally recognized form of marital/romantic relationships, as well as the ensuing ideals, norms, and pressures.

Non-monogamy versus polyamory: "Non-monogamy" is used either as (a) an umbrella term for everything other than monogamy or (b) to describe the act of having sexual but non-emotional relations outside of a primary relationship. The term "open relationship" is an example of the latter definition of non-monogamy; however, many people use all three names interchangeably. The phrase "two-plus-one" is more commonly used among gay men to refer to an agreement to have sexual encounters outside of a primary emotional commitment (Adam 2006). The term "polyamory" emphasizes not only the desire for multiple sexual and emotional connections, but also a philosophy and culture based on full disclosure, honesty, and non-possessiveness. Polyamory, as a word, gained popularity in the mid-1990s and has replaced non-monogamy to describe multiple emotional and sexual connections. "Consensual multi-partnering" is also used as an umbrella term for all forms of non-monogamy other than adultery (including polyamory, swinging, and open relationships). Notably, the use of "non-monogamy" prior to the popularization of polyamory included an implied potential for emotional connections with several people simultaneously, although this outcome did not always follow.

Primary/secondary: Some polyamorists place a hierarchy on their relationships, creating primary, secondary, and tertiary relationships. A person in a primary relationship may reserve certain acts for their primary partner and prioritize them in their day-to-day decision making. A secondary partner may be long term and emotionally significant but will come second in terms of important decision making and possibly time allocation. There may also be tertiary relationships, but if an individual has three lovers, both the second and third lovers are more likely to be considered secondary relationships. It should be noted that these words may be used in negotiation but are not usually used in common conversation or as terms of affection. Many polyamorists eschew hierarchies and thus will have two (or more) primary relationships in which each lover is treated more or less equally and not prioritized in decision making. In any of these situations, partners may be "in love" with their primary and secondary lovers. Primary does not necessarily denote the person one lives with, the co-parent of one's children, or the person who came first, although these are often qualities of the primary.

Polyfidelity and triad: With polyfidelity, three or more people may be involved in one relationship, which may also be called a group marriage, polyexclusivity, or a polyfaithful relationship. These people tend to be sexually and emotionally exclusive to the members of the group, with varying assortments of connections between them, and may or may not have lovers outside of their closed circle. In a triad (also known as a thruple), all three people are involved in one relationship with or without a required exclusivity outside this relationship, while a quad refers to four people in such a configuration. Another related term is "moresome," which Sheff (2006, 640) defines as "a relationship composed of five or more sexual and/or affective partners."

V-relationship: In a "V" formation, two people are involved with one person – the crux of the V. These people may also have lovers outside of the V, forming other Vs. In this case a "chain" of lovers is formed, sometimes called a "W."

Cohearts: Cohearts, also called metamours, are people who are both lovers with one particular person but are not lovers with each other (as in a V-relationship). The relationship between cohearts varies significantly, although they typically know each other and tend to be at least friendly acquaintances. The polyamorous ideal is to have harmonious, caring, and compersive relationships between cohearts.

Relating-ship: Polyamorists use the term "relating-ship" to refer to a relationship dynamic somewhere between romance and platonic friendship. This term illustrates the movement by polyamorists to challenge the dichotomy between lover and friend, and the mono-normative privileging of lover over friend, thereby allowing for a greater range of social/sexual interactions. It is also be used by some polyamorists to avoid creating a hierarchy of lovers (such as primary/secondary/tertiary), to emphasize the emotional significance of the connection, or to avoid the trivializing connotation of terms such as "friends with benefits" or "casual lover." This term may also connote a degree of acceptable flirting between people who are not necessarily in a formal relationship. (On a side note, in connection with blurring the divide between friend and lover, "It's complicated" tends to be a either a code for non-monogamy on social media sites or a euphemism for a less appealing form of monogamous relationship.)

Polyshagory: I coined the term "polyshagory" in an article in 2008[6] as a tongue-in-cheek way to distinguish between dating around with the intention of eventually becoming monogamous with one person and intentional polyamorous practice (i.e., longer-term emotional commitments with multiple people). The term helps to identify otherwise monogamous people casually dating multiple people compared to committed polyamorists.

Swingers: Swingers tend to be emotionally monogamous in a dyad and engage in sexually open practices on delineated occasions (sometimes meeting regularly over long periods of time) without developing emotional attachments to their sexual partners outside of the primary relationship. While there are exceptions within swinger culture, the men tend to be exclusively heterosexual, while the women are usually permitted to engage in sexual connections with other women. Swingers often refer to their practice as "the lifestyle" (see Gould 1999).

Swolly: "Swolly" refers to people who straddle both polyamorous and swinger identities and practice. The term was coined to complicate the divide that positions swingers as solely interested in recreational sex outside their relationship and polyamorists as being primarily interested in emotional connections. "Swolly" attempts to trouble the binary between sex and love within a sex-positive discourse and to recognize the overlap between the practices, communities, and discourse.

---

6   Jillian Deri, "Polyamory vs Polyshagory," *Daily Extra*, 12 February 2008, http://dailyxtra.com/vancouver/news/polyamory-vs-polyshagory.

Monogamish: Coined by popular syndicated columnist Dan Savage, "monogamish" refers to practices that are mostly monogamist but fall outside the bounds of its strict delineation in ways that are personalized by the couple. One example is a couple who is monogamous most of the time but welcomes casual short-term sexual encounters while one member of the couple travels. Such a couple may technically fall within the category of open relationship but might feel as though their more significant practice is that of their monogamist commitment to each other and that their openness is extraneous. Another example is a couple who is comfortable with flirting or kissing outside the relationship but is otherwise emotionally and sexually exclusive. Monogamish practices are likely informed by the burgeoning dialogue of polyamory and the increasing acceptance of open relationships. Another variant of monogamish is the concept of polyflexible. This term is likely a parallel to the term "homoflexible," used by people who are mostly heterosexual but are sometimes swayed to engage in same-sex acts when the opportunity is appealing.

Hook-up culture: Hook-up culture is an increasingly popular means for youth to engage in sexual encounters, often with multiple people in a mostly casual and temporary setting. There is disagreement as to whether this phenomenon ought to be considered a form of non-monogamy. However, there is significant overlap in regard to the notion that monogamy is not to be assumed after a sexual encounter and is instead to be negotiated.

Polyamorous Ideas of Jealousy

Polyamorous culture critiques mono-normativity and how it shapes emotional experiences of jealousy, love, and sexuality. It should be noted that there is a difference between the practice of monogamy and the institution of monogamy. Inclusive of polygamy, if one accounts for the prevalence of cheating (and somewhat less commonly, swinging), the practice of true monogamy is more atypical – both in Western culture and elsewhere (Barker and Langdridge 2010a; Duncombe et al. 2004; Kipnis 2004; Mead 1968; Ryan and Jetha 2010). Indeed, according to Barker and Langdridge (2010b, 752), "current relationships are generally monogamous in name rather than deed, non-consensual non-monogamy being a more common mode of relating." However, as the institution of monogamy is held up as the standard of true love, any breach of this practice is frowned upon. Therefore, if true love is framed as necessarily monogamous, breaching monogamy must inevitably lead to jealousy. Polyamorists work to remove the connection between love and sexual exclusivity, thereby attempting to disrupt the connection between jealousy and non-monogamy.

To the extent that popular culture equates jealousy with loss of control, polyamorous culture views jealousy as an emotion over which people have a great deal of control. Easton and Liszt (1997), the authors of the book *The Ethical Slut*, often considered the "Bible of Polyamory," contend that jealousy is not something that is caused by one's partner and therefore cannot be blamed on her/him. Instead, jealousy originates within the self and thus is one's own responsibility. By this argument, feeling jealous or behaving jealously will not change a partner's actions. Jealousy is portrayed at the same time as an internalized individual emotion and as socially constructed. The one who suffers most is the one feeling jealous, but such jealousy can also distress the other partner. Jealousy is an emotion that cannot be experienced in isolation; rather, it is representative of other feelings, such as low self-esteem, insecurity, or dissatisfaction with the relationship. Because jealousy is related to these unfavourable emotions, it is also linked to feelings of shame, which can prevent acknowledgment and mitigation of jealousy.

In his popular online essay, Veaux (2006) insists that within open relationships, jealousy needs to be addressed by looking at underlying emotional issues rather than by changing the actions that are the surface triggers of jealousy; otherwise patterns will repeat themselves. Author of the book *Opening Up*, Taormino (2008, 162) asserts that it is important to let yourself feel any remaining jealousy and validate whatever feelings you have, instead of "criticiz[ing] yourself or pil[ing] shame and judgment on top of it – that will just make you feel worse." In addition, Taormino maintains that one must believe that loving multiple people is possible in order to be successful in open relationships. She contends, "If you don't, you will always see other people and other relationships as infringing on and threatening to yours" (ibid., 158).

Easton (quoted in Klesse 2006b, 646) notes that the dominant strategy for dealing with negative emotions is avoidance and denial. She argues instead for a sociopolitical analysis of personal experiences of jealousy that encourages full expression of all emotions. According to the polyamorous model, feeling any emotion is appropriate, but acting on that emotion should be tempered with grace. Courtney framed it this way:

We have feelings. We choose how we act. We don't choose how we feel. So I would say, "there, there little feeling." But the feeling is like a kindergarten child. And I don't let kindergarten children drive my car.

Similarly, Francine stated, "There are not bad feelings. There are no bad thoughts. Just bad actions." Thus it may be acceptable to feel jealous, but it would not be appropriate to display the emotion by yelling vulgarities at one's partner, for example. In her polyamory self-help workbook, Labriola (2013, 74) suggests that polyamorous people need to rewrite popular beliefs about love and relationships. For example, there is a core myth that "if my partner really loved me, they wouldn't have any desire for a sexual relationship with anyone else." She rewrites this belief as, "My partner loves me so much that they trust our relationship to expand and be enriched by experiencing even more love from others" (ibid., 75). There is also a core belief that "it's just not possible to love more than one person at the same time" (ibid., 79). These myths are based on the idea of a "scarcity economy of love," which is easily refuted when one considers how people are able to love more than one child or friend at a time. Polyamorous people approach love as abundant and expandable. In a sense, monogamy remains normative because jealousy is assumed to be the natural and only possible reaction to a partner's extra-relationship practices.

Although the doctrine of compulsory monogamy does influence our experience of jealousy, emotions cannot simply be liberated from these dominant forces. Instead, following Weeks's (2008, 29) example, we must look at the

> historically shaped series of possibilities, actions, behaviours, desires, risks, identities, norms and values that can be reconfigured and recombined, but cannot be simply unleashed.

So while it is true that cultural regulation greatly affects our emotion world, agency also matters. Polyamorists attempt to manifest alternatives to jealousy by developing a different set of expectations than those implicit in dominant culture. The culture in which we live shapes our identity, and our understanding of this identity is somewhat limited by the language available (Weeks 2003). Whereas a monogamous cultural discourse has not identified a word for the opposite of jealousy, polyamorists have developed language to express occasions of pleasure ensuing from their non-monogamous practice: compersion. In what ways does naming an emotional practice increase the likelihood of its occurrence? If there was no word for jealousy or its opposite, might these emotions remain unexperienced?

Courtney remarked, "Queers do not have the luxury of leading an unexamined life ... And so it is for those of us who are sexually strange in some way." According to Heaphy, Donovan, and Weeks (2004), an unintended benefit of the historical exclusion of gays and lesbians from institutionalized marriage is that gays and lesbians have had ample opportunity to question the institution of marriage.[7] Through this reflexive critique, they have created relationship alternatives to the mainstream that often better reflect their chosen sexual expression, with a renewed importance given to pleasure, as opposed to an obligation to fulfil the expectations of others (ibid.). These creative alternatives include open relationships, the emotional dimension of polyamory, and the pursuit of compersion. I examine how these polyamorous ideas are actualized in ways that make embodied experiences of compersion possible and where these ideals fail to be realized. The discourse on polyamory calls into question compulsory monogamy and the presumed naturalness and inevitability of jealousy.

Compersion

The term "compersion" was coined by members of Kerista, a polyfidelitous commune in San Francisco (1971–91). The members of the Kerista commune defined compersion as

> the feeling of taking joy in the joy that others you love share among themselves, especially taking joy in the knowledge that your beloveds are expressing their love for one another.[8]

My participant Heloise described compersion this way:

> Being in a poly relationship doesn't mean you are okay with your partner being with other people. It means you are actually supportive of your partner being with other people. And that you are part of what makes that happen ... How could I not be happy if she is happy and having fun?

---

7   Notably, in Canada same-sex marriage has been legal since 2006, and thus this "unintended benefit" allotted to same-sex relationships is diminishing.

8   http://www.polyamorysociety.org/compersion.html.

Ryan and Jetha (2010) assert that non-monogamy has been the dominant practice throughout human history and that, historically, most non-monogamous sexual arrangements did not result in jealousy. It is possible that the experience of compersion was prevalent in such arrangements, but the term did not exist as such. Polyfidelitists and polyamorists were the first to coin the term and use it to describe a goal for their sexual relationships. According to Anderlini-D'Onofrio (2004, 4), the

> ability to turn jealousy's negative feelings into acceptance of, and vicarious enjoyment for, a lover's joy is a key operative concept in today's polyamorous practice.

One's experience of compersion can take many forms, ranging from tolerance to strong pleasure, and includes both non-sexual joy and sexual arousal. Compersion usually connotes one's response to a lover's happiness, but it could also be applied to joy in relation to the happiness of platonic friends or family. Indeed, experiencing compersion in a non-romantic context can be a stepping stone for understanding and extending this practice to romantic relationships.

The term "compersion" appears to have its roots in the word "compassion." As Francis (n.d.) states, "compersion is the compassion for the love pleasure of other people and compassion for your own pleasure and desire." Ferrer (2007, 37) suggests,

> Compersion can be seen as a novel extension of "sympathetic joy" that was developed within certain Buddhist philosophies, which is one of four immeasurable states or qualities of an enlightened person.

To understand compersion, he turns to a figure in Vajrayana Buddhism, the Goddess Green Tara, "who is said to have the power of turning jealousy into the ability to dwell in the happiness of others" (ibid., 40). Ferrer notes, however, that because many Buddhist teachings were developed by monks "who were not supposed to develop emotional attachments ..., the lack of systemic reflection in Buddhism upon romantic jealousy should not come as a surprise" (ibid.).

Polyamorous Critiques of Monogamy

Although they are often read in opposition to one another, monogamy and polyamory should not be approached as dichotomous. After all, many of the ideas out of which polyamory emerged come from the institution of monogamy. Also, ideas born out of polyamory are being adopted by people who are engaging in mostly monogamous relationships, as described earlier in regard to "monogamish." Monogamy is the central model in contemporary Western culture and the only legal option for marriage. The strict practice of monogamy, however, is far from the most common, and many functionally monogamous couples construct their own variation of this model by "violating the boundaries" (Ben-Ze'ev and Goussinsky 2008, 134). One contentious argument is that deviations from monogamous practice actually aid in the maintenance of the institution of monogamy. For example, having the option to cheat may contribute to a person's choice to stay in a long-term relationship. Ben-Ze'ev and Goussinsky (2008, 212) note that some people see "parallel relationships" (i.e., extramarital affairs) "as aiding and preserving their marriage" and that many people pursue such relationships without having any intention of leaving their marriage. They quote a participant who says, "The spark is alive and well in my marriage, but I think that's because seeing an adulterer makes me a more fulfilled partner."[9] Of course, I bring up this possibility not to condone cheating but rather to interrogate the limits of imposed sexual monogamy and the value of discussing alternatives.

In the polyamorous context, Heloise stated that while her wife was busy raising their children, their sex life had diminished, and her ability to have sexual encounters kept her devotion strong in her primary relationship. "I would have gone crazy. I mean, I don't know what I would have done if I could not have had sex and play stuff outside." Swingers likewise breach the bounds of monogamy but also reinforce monogamy's primacy through the invisibility of their trysts. In reality, while monogamy is still the cultural norm, there is a vast array of relationship options which reside somewhere between monogamy and polyamory (Ben-Ze'ev and Goussinsky 2008; Taormino 2008). It should also be noted that because most of us were raised in a monogamous culture, the vast majority of polyamorists have practised some form of monogamy in their dating life, be it temporarily or long term.

---

9   Dan Savage also provides plenty of evidence through examples of this claim within his popular syndicated sex advice column, *Savage Love*, which give credence to this highly contentious possibility.

As Mint (2007b) notes in his popular online blog,

> Also, let us not forget what polyamory is. The poly movement is a straight-out refutation of monogamy. Polyamory upends notions of what a proper relationship should be, obviating the need for the large and growing adultery-advice industry, reforming jealousy from a green-eyed monster into a tame housepet, jettisoning possessiveness and its attendant insecurity, and redefining words like fidelity, commitment, and marriage.

While in this statement Mint positions polyamory as a "straight-out refutation of monogamy," I believe that the movement challenges some but not the entirety of monogamy. In particular, I identify eight misconceptions (or commonly held assumptions) about monogamy and its role in the maintenance of social stability that are challenged within polyamorous discourse.

The first misconception is that monogamy mitigates jealousy. Jealousy is assumed to be an expression of a partner's care; it is linked to the idea that human nature is inherently competitive and to ideas about the scarcity of love. Instead, it is the institution and ideology of monogamy that exacerbates the prevalence and social impact of jealousy. Clearly, there are many instances of jealousy that occur within the practice and the attempted maintenance of monogamy. The culture of polyamory encourages the experience of compersion as a result of romantic and sexual connections outside of a relationship, while discouraging jealousy as a way to demonstrate care.

The second misbelief is that monogamy generates longevity. In her book *Against Love: A Polemic*, Kipnis (2004) reports that approximately half of US marriages end in divorce (and only 38% of married people say they are happy). Gould (1999) argues that swingers have increased satisfaction and thus longevity in their relationships. There has not been enough research on the longevity of polyamorous relationships to offer a comparison, but clearly monogamy alone does not cause couples to remain together. Arguably, longevity is not the best criteria for gauging the success of a relationship, and many polyamorists contend that relationships should be valued instead based on their degree of happiness and support (among other things). Martha argued, "We have this idea that monogamous equates a sense of security and yet 50% of marriages end in divorce. It's a very false sense of security."

The third fallacy is that fidelity is realized through monogamy. Judging from the quantity of cultural narratives on adultery and the limited mainstream attention given to open relationships, adultery appears to be more socially acceptable than honest non-monogamy. Kipnis (2004) compared statistics on infidelity and found that the data showed a range from 20% to 70% of people having cheated on their spouse (i.e., one member of the couple "straying" at least once). Kipnis (2004, 11) notes that the inconsistency and broad range of the statistics means that "you can basically select any statistic you like to support whatever position you prefer to take on the prevalence of such acts." I concur that because of the stigma surrounding affairs, statistics on infidelity are likely to be inaccurate, but the numbers are probably higher than those reported. Robinson (1997, 150) found that while many people "recognize[d] and condone[d] the inevitable failure of monogamy," they still paid lip service to it. Whether the stereotype that a greater percentage of men than women commit adultery is valid, there is a double standard wherein men's adultery is considered less severe than women's, whose sexuality is subject to more social control (Ryan and Jetha 2010). Notably, breaches of either sexual fidelity or longevity do not diminish the cultural belief in the institution of monogamy (Staudenmaier 2001). Ferrer (2007, 42) argues that "the history of monogamy is the history of adultery," after which he comically quotes H.H. Munro, who says monogamy is "the Western custom of one wife and hardly any mistresses."

Fourth is the myth that monogamy ensures the "future accessibility of an apparently or potentially scarce commodity of sexual intimacy" (Overall 1998, 6). This construct is connected to the idea of possession within a relationship and assumes that monogamy itself ensures the lasting quality of a relationship and the security that comes from having a partner. As noted in the statistics on divorce, coupled with the frequency of loveless long-term relationships, monogamy does not ensure such qualities. As well, the ideal of lasting love built into marital vows is contradicted by the common complaint of boredom stereotypically associated with long-term marriage.

Fifth is the misjudgment that it is only possible to have enough love and energy for one person. This myth is challenged when one considers the love a parent has for all their children or how one can love more than one friend or family member. Similarly, many people continue to love their ex-partners as well as their current lover(s). Most people find it easy to understand loving multiple friends and family members yet seem unable to apply the same standard when it comes to romantic love (Ryan and Jetha 2010).

The sixth assumption is that monogamy is natural and hence superior. Far from being natural, the institution of monogamy as we know it today, theorists have argued, is related to capitalist institutions which perpetuate the idea of possession, ownership, and material inheritance (Barker and Ritchie 2007; Munson and Stelboum 1999; Robinson 1997). Robinson (1997) explores how capitalist patriarchy has directly benefited from the nuclear family structure and from women's emotional and financial dependence on men. This myth of "naturalness" is also challenged when one considers that the vast majority of societies historically and cross-culturally have not practised monogamy as we know it today (West 1996). Ryan and Jetha (2010) challenge the naturalness of monogamy by looking to non-human species, demonstrating that sexual monogamy in the animal world is by far the exception. Notably, the work of Fausto-Sterling (2000) emphasizes the cultural construction of "human nature" itself, thus challenging any claim to naturalness in relationships.

Seventh, there is a false impression that monogamy ensures good parenting. This notion is directly related to the myth that monogamy is natural and superior. This view is so powerful that it has kept many polyamorists in the closet about their practice for fear of having their children apprehended (see Sheff 2013). It is parallel to the argument that only heterosexual couples make good parents, which has been used to argue against same-sex marriage or single parenting. To counter the claim that raising children outside the mainstream is more demanding, this challenge comes not from an inherent deficiency in the polyamorous family but rather from the social condemnation imposed by the same ideology that reinforces the superiority of monogamy.

Finally, there is the assumption that only monogamous love can be "true love." This idea is reinforced in the lyrics of many popular love songs, in literature, and in commercial media. This myth assumes that all other forms of love are invalid or lesser than, and it results in the belief that if one truly loved their partner they would not seek the attention of another person. Love, then, is a finite quantity that one has to compete for, and true love is both rare and constantly in danger of being usurped by another.

As these misconceptions demonstrate, institutionalized monogamy has not succeeded in fulfilling its intended social role. Jealousy remains rampant with often violent and destructive outcomes (Ben-Ze'ev and Goussinsky 2008). Cheating, divorce, and unhappy marriages continue to be common. While polyamory does not guarantee any of the positive qualities just listed, it does make for an interesting case study to explore alternative relationship structures and their emotional experiences. Most polyamorists do not advocate the abolition of monogamy.

Rather, they critique institutional monogamy with the goal of lessening the cultural dominance of mono-normativity.

Polyamory is a "burgeoning sexual story" (Ritchie and Barker 2006) that encompasses a philosophy, identity, practice, and politic, all of which are constantly evolving. Polyamory emerged partly in response to a critique of institutionalized monogamy and in reaction to individuals' desire for multiple partners, both of which relied upon a particular political and social context. Thanks to the connectivity of the Internet, polyamorous philosophy and practice has reached a tipping point of visibility[10] and is gaining media credibility and attention. At the heart of polyamory is a critique of institutionalized monogamy, the pursuit of compersion, the emergence of a culturally specific vocabulary, and the establishment of cultural forums. The practice of polyamory is likely to remain on the margins, but the influence of its philosophy is already being felt in mainstream culture.

---

10   Kenneth Haslam, quoted in Regina Lynn, "Internet Pushes Polyamory to Its 'Tipping Point,'" 29 February 2008, http://archive.wired.com/culture/lifestyle/commentary/sexdrive/2008/02/sexdrive_0229.

3 If You Move to the Rainforest, You've Got No Right to Complain about the Rain: From Polyagony to Compersion

In theory there is no difference between theory and practice. In practice, there is.

Yogi Berra

I think we are all growing and evolving. I think there is really a huge collective consciousness around jealousy right now. Especially with polyamory becoming more and more a topic of discussion. I think that there is movement happening in the collective.

Martha (study participant)

When their relationships encounter difficulty, some polyamorists half-joke that instead of practising polyamory, they are practising "polyagony," a term used to remind us that jealousy can sometimes be acutely painful. With the recognition that polyamory does indeed have its challenges, how and why do polyamorists work through this emotional pain? I begin this chapter with a description of the various expressions of jealousy among my participants. Then I discuss how polyamorists have re-imagined jealousy and have developed tools, strategies, and norms with the intention of facilitating compersion. To understand polyamorous norms, I examine the common themes of polyamorous practice that have emerged through my interviews. The tensions and contradictions within the polyamorous community become apparent as I document an illustrative moment of this rapidly blossoming culture.

Like most social norms, the feeling rules of polyamory are always in flux and are not always followed. The strategies in place to mitigate jealousy do not work for all polyamorists nor for all circumstances.

Also, many polyamorists choose not to follow their subculture's presumed norms. For this reason, and in order to determine polyamorous norms, I tease out the intersection between what polyamorists are doing and what they wish they were doing – that place where polyamorous theory meets practice. In other words, I investigate what they do to alleviate the emotive dissonance, Hochschild's (1979, 565) term to refer to the discrepancy between one's emotions and the feeling rules appropriate for the situation. Because jealousy is not the only difficulty in polyamory, I briefly address some of the other challenges to successful polyamory, including time pressures, parenting, and practising safer sex – acknowledging that each of these issues could fill a book of their own. Finally, to assure the reader that there is more to poly than processing, I conclude with a discussion of several reasons that polyamorists work through difficult emotions and the rewards of polyamorous practice.

Polyagony: Like Someone Else Is Driving the Bus

Love lights more fire than hate extinguishes.

Ella Wilcox

Among my participants, jealousy was most often described as a difficult, undesirable, and challenging emotion, yet also one that was tolerable, manageable, and temporary. Jealousy is inspired by different circumstances in polyamorous relationships than in monogamous relationships. In monogamy, jealousy is frequently triggered by suspicion of or actual infidelity. In polyamory, while cheating is possible, it is not typically under these circumstances that jealousy is most common. For polyamorists, sexual non-exclusivity is not enough reason to feel jealous; lying, on the other hand, is seen as much more dangerous to the relationship. Polyamorous practice exposes people to more direct opportunities to see their partner with other people, under consensual agreements.

For many people, emotions are experienced as if they are isolated and individual. However, the singularity of emotions is artificial. Emotions emerge not only from psychological manifestations but also from social interactions and their cultural context. Indeed, Sara Ahmed (2012, 40) argues that "we are moved by the proximity of others," or what she calls the drama of contingency. Jealousy cannot be experienced outside of social relationships. And yet jealousy can continue to be felt far after the end of the situation from which it arose. Recalling a memory of an experience when one felt jealous can result in the reoccurrence of the feeling. Also, imagining a scenario without it ever actually occurring can also inspire the feeling of jealousy, and the feeling cannot necessarily be halted even when one realizes it is solely imagination. La Rochefoucauld (1967, 451) observes that jealousy "does not always die with love." Embittered emotions often continue beyond the end of a relationship, and this is partly why jealousy in intimate relationships can make us feel so vulnerable. The emotional impact of an intimate relationship can be highly influential and have longer-lasting effects than the interactions during the relationship. It is also for this reason that the challenge of overcoming jealousy is so appealing for polyamorists.

Among my participants, even those who managed their jealousy well described the feeling as quite terrible. Brianna stated,

> It feels irrational. And angry, and I get a lot of physical symptoms, like my heart beats fast and I get shaky and I get a little dizzy and I don't tend to have that kind of eruption of feeling with much else.

Alyson described jealousy in the following way:

> It feels like someone has taken over the inside of your head and is going to control your thought processes and keeps feeding advertising messages in there and I was having a perfectly normal time and now, screech! Oh, here's another thing to think about that is going to make you upset. It feels pretty out of control. Not being who I want to be and not feeling very calm. Feeling really reactive and feeling like someone else is driving the bus, which then makes me angry. Or a variety of other people are driving the bus but I am not anywhere close to the wheel.

Grace described jealousy in this way:

> Like a gross squishy feeling in your heart. I just picture my heart as really black and not functioning. Most of the time I just feel like I am so full of love or whatever that it's so fine, but when I'm jealous I just get tunnel vision and I'm crazy because I'm very obsessive actually. So I will think only of the person I'm jealous about and my partner and make up these situation in my mind to the point where if I don't get it out quick enough, I almost can't distinguish between what actually happened and what I've made up.

Orion said jealousy

> feels kind of like a closing door that I'm trying not to look through. I'm like, I don't want to see it, and I'm closing the door, and I kind of do want to see it, but I kind of don't. I get angry.

The range of metaphors used to describe jealousy demonstrates that jealousy is not a universal experience. Rather it is a culturally specific, complex mixture of emotion, feeling, and affect, informed by language. Some people experience anxiety when confronted with a challenge; others when confronted with this same challenge tend to experience stress, anger, withdrawal, or sadness. And quite possibly, jealousy has parallel emotional sensations to hate. Imagination can shift our memory of a situation and thus also our emotional experience, explaining why jealousy arises from actual or potential scenarios. There is also a discrepancy that occurs when affect is translated into words. Articulation is not always adequate for the preverbal ways jealousy is affectively experienced. Yet these descriptions provide an important context within which to understand the impact of jealousy and its reframing. Reddy (1999, 271–2) argues that instead of speaking of managing or constructing emotions, a more apt description is "navigation" because "navigation includes the possibility of both radically changing course and making constant corrections in order to stay on a chosen course."[11]

In her work on jealousy and polyamory, Labriola (2013) contends that jealousy can manifest in a variety of forms, including fear, anger, betrayal, hurt, anxiety, sadness, paranoia, loneliness, self-loathing, embarrassment, powerlessness, inadequacy, feeling excluded, and feeling disrespected. The shame associated with jealousy's tie to low self-esteem, insecurity, and immaturity can exacerbate the pain. It may be for this reason that many of my participants found ways to talk about the spectrum of jealousy using a variety of other terms. Nora called it "grungy feelings." Dominique called it "being stuck in a knot." Two participants talked about the "Committee of Assholes" to refer to the voices in their heads that told negative, jealousy-inducing stories.

---

11   Reddy (1999, 271–2) continues, "But even 'navigation' implies purposive action, whereas changes of goals are only purposive if they are carried out in the name of higher-priority goals."

Francine stated, "It would be a bunch of jerks in the back of his head going mememememe, him feeding himself a line of shit."

Jealousy for Orion was linked to embarrassment and made her inclined to withdraw: "maybe I would peel back some of the hearty stuff. Build a little fortress around my heart before it gets blood inside it." Tianna described jealousy as linked to a desire to control a situation, and she would ask many questions to gain control over her feelings. Jealousy is also significantly intertwined with fear. For Priscilla, "I think jealousy is often times about fear, fear of being left or not being able to control what's going on." Cheyenne responded, "What jealousy really comes down to is a fear of being replaced." For Nora,

> Usually what it comes down to is fear … Because I have a lot of fears. Like a lot of people do. Fear of inadequacy. Fear of abandonment. Fear of not being good enough in general. Once I can see those for what they are, which is simply fear. Fear is something that evolutionarily is really useful, but I think in those contexts it's less useful.

Polyamorists tend to describe jealousy and compersion as opposites, where their feelings occur as a matter of degree, ranging from extreme emotional pain, subtle twinges, and tolerance to delight and everything in between. However, jealousy and compersion are not necessarily oppositional and can occur simultaneously. Jealousy can play an important role without necessarily becoming compersion, such as by intuiting problems or guiding people to seek what they are lacking.

From Polyagony to Compersion: Norms, Etiquette, Tools, and Strategies

Jealousy is a dog's bark which attracts thieves.

Karl Kraus

Polyamorists "do … not remain stuck in deconstruction but dare to actively construct" (Haritaworn, Lin, and Klesse 2006, 518). Polyamorists actively develop polyamorous philosophy which contributes to their emotional experience associated with relationships, jealousy, and love – in both positive and negative ways. There is an interesting contradiction in the polyamorous community. On the one hand, jealousy is seen as something to which polyamorists need to give particular attention – they need to be proactive and up front in managing jealousy and therefore good at its mitigation. On the other hand, several polyamorists in my study reported a certain pressure to be "over it already," and this pressure actually stood in the way of mitigating jealousy since it drove it underground. Coraline called this "the posturing of poly cool." Several participants offered a rendition of the sentiment that "jealousy is socially constructed by the monogamy-centric mainstream culture" and thus should not be part of their poly experience. They felt that if they chose polyamory, they could not complain about how hard it could be. Heloise made this analogy: "If you move to the rainforest, you've got no right to complain about the rain." When polyamorists feel pressure not to be jealous, they often do not talk about their challenges, and this gives the false impression that everything is easy.

In this sense, these polyamorists are engaging with what Kenney and Craig (2012, 86) call "illegitimate pain," which refers to situational types of pain that are kept hidden "for fear of possible consequences," such as stigma or shame from within the polyamorous community. They argue that illegitimate pain tends to be "stigmatized as deviant or deserved" by one's social group (ibid., 88), and it is "the suffering brought about when individuals internalize, subject themselves to, or are subjected to moral codes that are in conflict with embodied emotional experiences" (ibid., 89). Jealousy then is a kind of suffering that might not garner sympathy from one's polyamorous peers and might foster a "what do you expect" reaction from their monogamous peers, or what they call "just punishment" (ibid., 90). In this sense, shame for feeling the inappropriate pain is added to the mix of emotionality, along with disappointment, frustration, or failure in connection to their gap between theory and practice.

As Ahmed (2012, 49) argues, "Disappointment can also involve an anxious narrative of self-doubt," such as in one's ability to practise polyamory. Rihanna noted the pressures from both the monogamous and polyamorous world views, yet the positive possibilities emerging from poly discourse as well:

> In the monogamous world, you are told you are supposed to be jealous of your mate. In poly, you are told you are not supposed to be jealous of your mate, so it's a different thing where being jealous is not considered an acceptable notion. Being jealous is not enforced or approved of. Then it becomes a small shameful act. Oh my God, I shouldn't be jealous. I should be all loving and compersiony and all that kind of stuff. And you do. So in

some ways it makes it harder to deal with because you are experiencing
something you are not supposed to experience, but in other ways it makes
it easier because you haven't got people reinforcing the jealousy for you.

Such pressures, however, were far from universal. Courtney was critical
of any restrictions or cultural norms established by a poly community:

I am not a straight girl, I did not grow up to be vanilla, I did not grow up to
be monogamous, and I did not remake my life so I could follow somebody
else's rules. Whether those be interesting or enticing, or the most wildly
box in the world, it is still a box. So poly community, I give not a fig.

Thus, while Courtney was aware of potential pressures from within the
polyamorous community, she did not feel affected by them, nor did she
feel obliged to participate.

Polyamorists are aware of the misconceptions and prejudice surrounding non-monogamy, such as that polyamorists are commitment-
phobic, promiscuous, or idealistic. When talking to monogamous
people about their relationships, polyamorists sometimes downplay
the challenges of being polyamorous, in an attempt to avoid adding
the stigma of experiencing jealousy to the stigma of being poly. Polyamorists work hard to dispel these negative stereotypes and therefore
may gloss over the polyamory challenges that could leave them open
to criticism (Klesse 2007). In addition, some polyamorous people downplay the sexual component of their relationships, emphasizing instead
the importance of the emotional connection in a (somewhat successful)
attempt to gain mainstream credibility, an approach that tries to appeal
to a sex-negative culture (Mint 2007b).

The culture of polyamory emerged in part as a resistance to the hegemonic structure of jealousy encapsulated in mono-normativity (Klesse
2006a; Mint 2007a). Whether poly people as a whole have achieved the
intended compersive intimacy is debatable, but polyamorous culture does
provide an interesting framework for developing personalized relationship structures which may cater to individualized emotional needs.
Polyamorists share the belief that it is possible to love more than one
person romantically and offer an opposition to the dominant monogamous model of love. Polyamorists tap into shared resources (websites,
workshops), ideas, and friendship circles, and they actively create their
own language and etiquette. Polyamorous culture rejects the notion
that jealousy is inevitable and intolerable. The culture of polyamory
challenges several ideals of monogamy and romantic love. It rejects the

romantic ideal of "total devotion," wherein true love must have only one object, and that true love lasts forever (Ben-Ze'ev and Goussinsky 2008). Polyamorists are critical of ideas of possession, ownership, or entitlement regarding a lover (Robinson 1997), which are often properties associated with envy (see Simmel 1955). Polyamorists see having multiple loves as a more realistic, rather than idealistic, expression of love. They claim that jealousy may be a "natural" part of a relationship yet also say it need not be there at all in relation to a lover's other sexual encounters.

One polyamorist norm is to differentiate and disconnect the source of jealousy from the event. The source of jealousy is understood to be one's own insecurities or monogamous socialization, as opposed to the presence of another lover. When jealousy does arise, polyamorists try to address the emotion rather than the event that "caused" the jealousy. Ideally, polyamorists support their lovers to mitigate adverse emotions, although the individual is ultimately responsible for their own emotional experience. For example, polyamorists will support their partners by offering reassurance or "being extra sweet," as Tianna called it, but will still go on a date with their other lover.

While polyamorists support each other by processing adverse emotions, to many polyamorists, the ultimate responsibility for one's emotional experience is a personal one. Tianna talked about how she would become jealous when her partner took another lover for a walk on the beach. She later realized that it was not the act of beach walking that was the problem; rather it was what it represented, which was intimacy of the girlfriend kind. She wanted to be the only one with that particular girlfriend status. By figuring out what the act represented to her, she was able to strategize other ways to feel primary, to reserve some activities as special and only for the two of them, and thus overcome the association of beach walks with jealousy.

Frequently stated in polyamorous culture is the idea that nobody can cause another person to feel jealous, that people are responsible for their own emotional experience. If this idea is taken too far, what emerges is a hyper-individuality. While this reflects a powerful agency over one's own emotions, it also underestimates the ways in which people are affected by the actions and words of others, or what Ahmed (2012, 47) calls "affective contagion." This notion applies to how polyamorists might feel joy or pain as their lovers experience joy or pain. Just as one might experience compersion when a lover has new relationship energy, so too might a polyamorist experience pain while a lover goes through a break-up.

Dominique described how protective she felt of her partner when she was going out on dates:

> You are going to put your life in someone else's hands. I would have to know for sure that that person was sane and armed in an appropriate way. I would have a very difficult time going to their home and looking at them. Are you going to hurt my Leigh? If I thought anyone was going to hurt you I would just kill them. I mean … the she-bear would just show up in a way you don't even want to know!

Notably, affective contagion is not mimicry and is contingent on what else is occurring, since clearly schadenfreude is also a possible outcome of one's lover's break-up, or one could feel embarrassment regarding the behaviour of an ex-lover.

Even though polyamorists claim that the ultimate responsibility for mitigating jealousy resides with the individual, ethical polyamory presupposes supporting one's partners when they experience jealousy. This is done mostly by reassuring, listening, and renegotiating boundaries. Priscilla supported her partner by taking things slow:

> Sometimes just backing down with whatever I was doing. Sometimes, for example, going painfully slow with somebody else while my partner has time to digest. Sometimes it's maddeningly slow, but I'm being good.

Tianna described how she supported her partner:

> So I made adjustments all along for her. I tried to give her lots of love. Lots of affection and lots of reassurance and lots of telling her I appreciate her and telling her I love her. Just kind of being extra sweet is how I define it. Thanking her for letting me do this stuff. Trying to appreciate her as a whole.

The jealousy of one's partner, in the previous two examples, was seen as a barrier to actualizing secondary polyamorous relationships, but it was resolved through support and negotiation.

According to Buss (2000), an evolutionary psychologist, jealousy in monogamy functions as a tool to intuit/identify a partner's cheating, show devoted love, and therefore prevent the partner from straying. In contrast, because polyamorists encourage encounters outside the relationship, jealousy functions more like a barrier than a tool for the full actualization of polyamorous love. Polyamorists want to trust their partners to play outside of the relationship, want their partner to have a good time doing so, want them to return afterwards, and they want everyone to feel compersion throughout this process. Because cheating and loss is still possible in polyamorous situations, however, Buss's description of the role of jealousy is still partly applicable. Brianna spoke of the "ultimate poly betrayal" – a partner having unsafe sex with another lover. She noted that her jealous intuition that he was doing so was "crazy-making," particularly because her partner responded to her suspicion as if she was just being insecure. In this case, the polyamorous ideal of addressing the emotion instead of the event did not serve her well. The distinction between suspicion and fait accompli jealousy is relevant here.

My participants described many instances of non-responsible practice under the guise of polyamory, many of which came from stories involving their ex-partners or stories about the experience of others. Celia acknowledged, "So being polyamorous didn't mean I was necessarily checking my crap any more than someone who has never been." Francine witnessed the following:

> I think people get really high off new relationships and totally fuck up something that is really meaningful and has layers and layers of love and history built in there and they get super excited. Or they use poly to segue out of a relationship that they are not happy in and start something new.

In this quotation, Francine described two unethical approaches to polyamory: when people compromise a prior relationship because they get caught up in the limerence of a new connection and when people use the guise of "opening up" to demote the relationship.

Clearly, freedom to have multiple sexual relationships does not necessarily guarantee trustworthy or ethical behaviour. Alyson noted that in her 20 years of poly experience, she met several people who stated non-monogamy as their preference but who were actually more interested in serial monogamy with overlaps at the end of one relationship and the beginning of another. Thus the desire to "see other people" was used as a (potentially cowardly) mechanism to leave the relationship. Because of this history, Alyson remained suspicious of people who espoused non-monogamy, and she remained a sceptic. Even though she continued to practise polyamory, this influenced her expectations and thus her experience of jealousy. For example, Alyson would always ask a lover to explain what she meant by polyamory when she chose the term and would increase trust by paying attention to actions rather than words. The reality that one's partner may leave one for another person is not avoided just because one has consented to their dating. There is nothing that guarantees longevity or commitment in polyamory any more than in monogamy. Notably, longevity is not in itself an accurate measure of the success of a relationship. Also, the fact that a relationship ended does not necessarily mean that it was a failure. However, this belief alone does not make break-ups emotionally easier for polyamorists. And a painful break-up can still taint the memory of the whole relationship.

There is a validity to the aphorism, "you do not get what you deserve, you get what you negotiate." Negotiation is central for the cultivation of compersion and intimacy, as well as for practical matters such as development of relationship rules. Polyamorists attempt to nurture a feeling of "specialness" in each relationship by creating or identifying an aspect that is unique to a particular couple within a configuration (Jamieson 2004). Whereas monogamous people often depend on sexual exclusivity to maintain a feeling of specialness, polyamorists find other ways to achieve this. Among poly couples where there is a primary/secondary hierarchy, they may negotiate reserving particular things for their primary relationship, such as acts (often sex acts), certain locations (their bed, for example), or certain time restrictions ("be home by 2 a.m.," "only one date a week," etc.). Heloise had only one rule in her relationship: "don't do anything you'd be ashamed of."

Another site for negotiation is rules of disclosure. Some examples of these are "tell me only the necessary details," "tell me before you do anything," "tell me within 24 hours after an act," and "tell me all the juicy details." Orion had a three-question agreement, where her partner could ask her three questions about a date, thus putting the control of information sharing into her partner's hands. Her partner could opt to hear more banal information (such as "what did you have for dinner?") or choose more intimate questions. After the three questions, she could decide whether or not she wanted to hear more. Francine refused rules and instead would only offer considerations. She argued that rules were a form of control, but giving consideration to one's partner involved knowing what she would want and finding the place where her partner's needs met her own, thus coming from a place of respect rather than obligation.

The clear communication and negotiation necessary for polyamory to operate smoothly can be challenging and can provoke a great deal of vulnerability in many people. The option to negotiate preferences and parameters does not necessarily translate to a compersive outcome. There are situations where no satisfactory compromise can be reached by all parties. Courtney spoke of one lover agreeing to a polyamorous situation but then imposing several arbitrary and hard-to-achieve rules, making another relationship virtually impossible. When she expressed her jealousy, Tianna's partner would sometimes respond with frustration and anger: "then my partner will become pissed off and angry and think I'm a control freak and think that I'm trying to sabotage her date. And that ain't pretty." Although trust is necessary for the success of polyamory, honesty is not a given, even when one is committed to disclosing and negotiating strong rules and boundaries.

Among my interview subjects, honesty was highly valued, but full disclosure was rarely practised and rarely idealized. Over-sharing was often seen as disrespectful since it led to "dumping" information onto people who may or may not have wanted to know certain details. This practice is reflected in William Blake's clever observation: "A truth that's told with bad intent beats all the lie you can invent." Thus, there is a crucial distinction between honesty and full disclosure. For example, a polyamorist may be happy to know that her lover is doing well with other lovers but may not want to hear the details of her partner's sexual adventures. Full disclosure may be considered disrespectful and rather rude. Polyamorous etiquette indicates that pertinent information should be offered willingly and without one needing to pry it out of a partner, but what counts as pertinent is variable. Some examples of what polyamorists want to know are the quantity of time they spent together, emotional affections (how much do you like her?), or an issue to which they are particularly sensitive (often about their sexual connection).

In polyamorous culture, as Orion eloquently stated, "it's not sleazy to hit on someone's partner." Poly etiquette suggests that it is okay to flirt with or pursue a person who has a known partner. When one does so, they are not seen as trying to "steal" one's date, as long as they follow proper etiquette. Such etiquette involves demonstrating respect, clarity, and open communication regarding intentions towards the person with whom one is flirting and their partner(s). Etiquette also suggests that a person devote their full attention to the person (or people) with whom they are on a date. Flirting with other people is usually not done at this time. When polyamorists neglect these subtle social graces, however, others feel disrespected and compersion is difficult. It is important to note that flirting means different things in different cultural contexts.

For example, Martha stated, "In my circle of friends, we flirt, we touch." Among polyamorists, flirting does not necessarily represent the desire to replace but may express playfulness, appreciation, friendship, or romantic interest, the subtleties of which are significant yet not always apparent. Indeed, many femmes flirt with their platonic friends as an affectionate way of socializing and bonding.

Given the small size of many poly communities, especially among queer-leaning individuals, overlaps of friends and lovers are quite common. Overlapping social networks could be a catalyst for jealousy, but polyamorous people have established an etiquette that minimizes difficult emotions through upfront discussion. In this instance, poly-amorous etiquette calls for people to communicate with all the people who may be adversely affected by a relationship, including friends and ex-lovers. Etiquette calls for them to ask for permission or act in a way that would minimize jealous tensions. For example, when Alex started dating a new person, she got in touch with the new partner's ex (who was an acquaintance) to check in about boundaries and prefer-ences. Tianna identified one "unwritten expectation" wherein it was the coheart's responsibility to introduce herself to the primary and initiate dialogue, "so I can receive you in my court." Most participants relied on other polyamorous people for relationship support and were par-ticularly caring and accountable to each other. In regard to the small community of lesbians, Courtney remarked,

> We really have to spend a lot of time to make sure we get our shit on straight. And we need to try harder to get along with each other and we have to try harder to behave ethically towards each other because there isn't enough room in a small community to have great big drama and then safely move away from it.

For these reasons, polyamorous people widen the boundaries of their poly family to include lovers, ex-lovers, close friends, and intimate non-sexual friends, treating them all with consideration as one might a romantic relationship. Polyamorists are generally critical of the mono-normative tendency of the "privileging of love relationships over oth-ers" (Barker and Langdridge 2010a, 4). Significantly, close friendship and mutual respect often formed between cohearts, and often between ex-lovers of one's partner. Cheyenne lived with her family of lovers and her child. This family included three people who either have been or are lovers to her, and she said,

The connections are all there in terms of being committed to each other and being responsible for one another, and supporting each other's foundation at the end of the day ... We are definitely a family unit. All the connections aren't necessarily sexual ones but they are strong bonds regardless.

Celia once lived with her partner and coheart, about whom she said, "One thing I like about polyamory is the recognition that there are many kinds of intimate committed ways to be close to someone," by which she meant a familial connection, beyond simply friends and lovers. However, she soon followed up that comment with this remark:

There were also moments of a lot of unspoken tension and difficulty, and of course we would never compete for the person's attention, ever, ever ever! [*said with a sarcastic tone*] It was trickier because there were always two people wanting the same thing from someone.

There is often an expectation that a friendship should emerge after a break-up. Although this expectation is common, such friendships are not always possible. Some study participants observed pressure to be friends with their exes and were concerned about how it looked to their community when such a friendship did not emerge. One participant even used a person's relationship with their significant exes as a measure of the ability to be in polyamorous relationships.

Celia is a participant who identified with and practised both monogamy and polyamory, stating that her preference shifted over time depending on the dynamic with her lover(s). She noted that in her poly relationships, it was common for her partner to check in with her about whether it is okay to flirt with a certain person. This act of requesting consent included her in the decision, which mitigated the potential for jealousy. Her monogamous partners, however, did not think to check in about flirting given that it was not supposed to exist in their dynamic and such boundaries were assumed rather than discussed. According to Celia, it was this exclusion from the decision-making process that triggered her jealousy. She also noted that in a polyamorous dynamic, a partner's crush could potentially become a new relationship, whereas in a monogamous coupling, the fear was that her partner may leave her entirely for another person. In monogamous connections, she said, "I also find that I am more likely to worry if my partner has a fancy that I can't meet." Tianna argued that if a crush remained unexplored because it was taboo, it would likely blossom. When a sexual act is forbidden or repressed, there tends to be an increase in desire to speak about it as well as an increase in the pleasure acquired from violating these taboos. If a partner is permitted to explore a crush, they are likely to "get it out of their system" and find a better balance. In both of these cases, practising polyamory worked to decrease instances of jealousy.

Among my participants, the process around acts was often as important as the acts themselves in the mitigation of jealousy. When Tianna's partner was going out on a date with a new person, she felt a twinge of jealousy. She did not ask her partner to forgo the date but instead asked for an opportunity to express her feelings, to receive confirmation of her importance, and then bid them an evening farewell with a smile. Neither partner appraised the date as the source of jealousy; rather, the source was insecurity or fear. In contrast, Brianna stated that her monogamous friends felt jealousy in situations that "a polyamorist would not even notice," such as a partner looking at another person. Cheyenne noted that jealousy was different for monogamous and poly people because there was a different construction of the boundaries of a relationship:

> I talk to people all the time who say, "my boyfriend looked at another woman and I don't even want to know about it!" … I can support that, I can hear that's really hard for you, but I can't understand it.

Cheyenne found this acceptance of a range of attractions outside the relationship to be one cultural difference between polyamorists and some monogamists. Similarly, Heloise commented on an example of her monogamous heterosexual friend; she said that "if her man even looked at somebody else, she would become physically sick for a week. Just looked at another women! You've thrown me for a complete loop!" She noted that this friend's monogamy did not prevent the upsurge of jealousy. Polyamorists tend to look down on this kind of possessiveness.

There were instances where my participants described their jealousy in a way that is consistent with Freud's theory of projection, a guilt not that we suspect our partner's infidelity but that we ourselves want to cheat, either through outside affairs or by breaking a rule. Orion noted that the bulk of her monogamous breaks-ups were due to "developing affections for other people." While practising poly eliminated the necessity of breaking up when there was a new lover or attraction, the projected fear of being left by a partner for this reason persisted. Tianna also experienced projected jealousy and found that trust was more difficult when NRE or one's sexual drive got in the way. Tianna simultaneously spoke of her own experience and what she projected onto her partner.

> I do for the most part trust her in that regard, like 97% of the time. Some-
> times new relationship energy gets in the way. Sometimes your dick gets
> in the way. What happens when you really like her? I had a little bit of that
> with Blaire [Tianna's secondary date], so this is a little hypocritical.

She also noted that it was easier to trust a partner when other components of the relationship felt strong. When things were difficult, she
feared that her partner would leave her for the new person, with whom
things were still light and easy. Sometimes the desire was as much
about attraction to an outside person as it was about a desire to break a
rule. For Priscilla,

> If I'm not supposed to do it then it's really hot. It's sort of a weakness ...
> Well, it made it more hot for me, in that sort of secret, forbidden, taboo-y
> sort of way, which was totally not forbidden ... But it's my rules. That's the
> thing, sticking to my rules and respecting the agreements you have with
> people. That's the most difficult part.

Priscilla exemplified a feature common in polyamorous discourse,
which is a refusal to be confined by the imposition of dominant and
seemingly arbitrary rules. A sense of agency and resistance to mono-
normative values is often important to polyamorists. Such resistance is
itself one of the reasons some people choose to engage in polyamory.
The pursuit of being in control of emotions, of sexuality, and of one's
relationship model at times seems to have as much to do with a political
opposition or status in a subculture as with a personal desire. This aspect
of polyamorous choice corresponds to the "posturing of poly cool" in
that poly is perceived in some limited circles as being progressive and as
something to be practised by those who are more "emotionally evolved."
Such an association of poly with a progressive political stance must be
contrasted with marginalization felt by polyamorists in other circles. In
other words, some polyamorists exhibit a defensive celebration of their
practice in response to dominant culture's criticism of it. Political or
philosophical motivations (or both) for engaging in polyamory make
for different experiences of jealousy than do emotional or desire-based
motivations. If one truly wishes to be in a polyamorous situation, that
person may find it easier than someone who believed in the philosophy
and wished for compersive emotions to follow accordingly.

There is a joke about polyamory that sums up one apprehension about
the lifestyle: how many polyamorists does it take to screw in a light

bulb? None; they are too busy processing to screw.[12] In other words, polyamory is a lot of work. Celia noted, "Polyamory can be wonderful, amazing, life-enriching, can bring you amazing, life-enriching things. Simplicity is never one of them." Similarly, Francine said this about poly: "At least it is never boring." The idea that relationships take work is so pervasive that it often goes unquestioned (Kipnis 2004). Add more relationships into the mix and there will be more work (Taormino 2008).

Katz (2012, 6) coined the term "crucible of emotions" to refer to "the work people do in aligning actions with the habits, routines, and movements of others." For polyamorists, this crucible of emotions includes communication, processing, negotiation, and self-reflection, often geared towards reducing jealousy. The understanding is that jealousy should never be dealt with in a violent fashion, in opposition to popular representations that portray reactions to jealousy using anger and aggression. There is an expectation of non-violent communication, which refers to the use of language that emphasizes empathy, clarity, and compassion instead of "violent" language of coercion or manipulation.[13] Polyamorous culture encourages clarity and upfront communication, in particular about attraction to other people, intentions in a relationship, and sexual practices. Although not unique to polyamory, an unintended benefit of such communication is a great depth of intimacy, feeling of freedom, and a sense of interdependence in a relationship. Several participants reported feeling closer to their polyamorous partners than they had felt to their past monogamous partners. In their study on swingers, De Visser and McDonald (2007) also found that the processing swinging couples did to minimize jealousy strengthened their intimate connection. Francine was particularly upfront about negotiating boundaries and consent. She recalled the following story:

> We ended up being in this big chain of people and … one of the people had a managed [sexually transmitted] disease that no one had bothered to tell me about and I felt kind of like, Hey, I would really like to know what I'm getting into and I felt like that wasn't fair. So I called a meeting with everybody, so there was eight people at my house for dessert and I just said we

---

12   Another variation of this joke is that polyamorists are too busy scheduling to screw.
13   Non-violent communication was adopted from Marshall Rosenberg's (2003) conflict resolution strategy.

need to decide how we are going to handle this ... Let's all discuss what's going on. I would like to feel that I get to make the decision around it.

This kind of upfront clarity builds trust, which is crucial for mitigating jealousy. Direct processing may seem like more work in the beginning, but my study participants agreed that it brought a greater depth of intimacy to their relationships and essentially made polyamory possible for the long term.

All of my participants agreed that communication was the central tool for mitigating jealousy and enabling compersion. Communication involves negotiating boundaries (which are never a given), learning and expressing one's own triggers for jealousy, and building trust. Some participants felt that the vulnerability that comes from discussing one's jealousy was emotionally risky. Through practising polyamory, however, jealousy was normalized and thus minimized. Rihanna argued that "the three C's of poly are Communicate, Communicate, Communicate." For instance, one participant noted that as soon as she vocalized her feeling of jealousy and had it heard, the feeling dissipated. Grace relayed the following:

I get it out as soon as humanly possible ... We try to figure out if there is something tangible we can do to make the feelings stop. Do you need more attention? Do you just need me to listen to you? I need to get all the crazy crap out so I can hear myself say out loud and hear how completely ridiculous it is ... I am not into denying my jealousy ... One of my yoga instructors said, whenever she felt jealous she would tell whoever she was jealous of that she was jealous at the first opportunity that she could, and she found that the other person usually took it as a compliment and that diffused the situation a little bit. It was easier for her to feel this bad feeling when it was actually making someone else feel good, but at the same time there was no power because the other person couldn't use the jealousy over her because it was out there in the open.

Interestingly, she also described how it can feel good when someone is jealous of you, and in a sense there was even a compersive attitude of feeling good because she made another person feel good as a result of her own jealousy.

In contrast to Grace's story, other participants felt that this kind of vulnerable exposure was emotionally risky and did not lead to the same result. Alyson observed that having space to experience her feelings and speak her mind only sometimes dissipated negative emotions:

> I've spent time with lovers of my girlfriend. Sometimes that works, some-
> times it doesn't. I think what matters is for me to be allowed to let my feel-
> ings run their course and not feel like I'm being corralled into something.
> If I don't necessarily like somebody, I don't want to feel pressured to like
> them. I like to figure out what I think of them. Just because you like them
> doesn't mean that I'm going to like them. I need to be able to take my own
> time. That matters to me about being given that.

Notably, most polyamorists found that liking their coheart eased feelings of jealousy and built their sense of trust, and vice versa; the more
trust they had, the more they would like their cohearts. Many participants also noted that allowing yourself to feel whatever you felt rather
than forcing or repressing the emotion was a useful strategy to mitigate jealousy. In contrast, Nora said, "I don't let emotions run me." In
this instance, Nora was suggesting a common Western notion of controlling emotions as a means of assuaging negative feelings. The extent to
which emotions can be controlled, either at the stage of affect or the stage
of expression, varies significantly among individuals and will be further
examined in chapter 4 in the context of a gender analysis.

Orion noted, "Jealousy is the beginning, not the end of something."
In other words, jealousy can be an opportunity to investigate one's
emotional needs rather than a reason to stop one's actions. It should
be noted that not all polyamorists have primary relationships with secondary dates on the side; however, among those who did, the arrival
of a new lover frequently coincided with the emergence of a jealous
episode. Another instance that provoked jealousy was when a partner's
date moved from a place of novelty into actual love. Dominique said,

> The challenging part is not the new relationship energy, it's the real life
> experience. It's not so much the early hot sex. It's the falling in love that
> gets me in trouble.

Many participants found that lack of information about a partner's
new lover was worse than the known information. Nora said, "When I
don't know who they are, they turn into this giant bogeyman." In other
words, imagining the fabulousness of the new lover was worse than

knowing them personally, since one's imagination tends to construct grander images than actually exist. Tianna said,

> I've found that some of the hardest stuff to work through is bumping up against boundaries that you didn't know were there until you hit them … That can be tricky, because if you didn't know the boundary was there, it wasn't intentional but the hurt is already there. Like it's already done, so trying to unpack some of that and trying to unravel that without my partner getting defensive or feeling attacked or whatever can be challenging.

In other words, negotiating boundaries only took her so far because the events that caused her the most strife could not be predicted. Other times, the recognition that a troubling act was not done with malicious intent can ease the hurt.

The assumption that jealousy must be inevitable in a given situation, as frequently modelled in compulsory monogamy, contributes to the feelings of jealousy. Thus, re-crafting the model of love and relationships also shifts the experience of jealousy. Here is an example of how monogamy as an institution relates to jealousy, an example that may be polemic but is still a common narrative. A tabloid headline read "Madonna's A-Rod Jealousy Plan." The article claimed that Madonna was spending time with a young model, Jesus, to make her long-term lover (Alex Rodriguez, or A-Rod) jealous. The expectation was that Alex would inevitably feel jealous from such an action. The article assumed that a person can make someone else feel jealous and that creating jealousy was a controlled strategy to bring her a certain result (such as a commitment from Alex). This suggests too that the use of the word "jealousy" is removed from any real feeling, since reports did not come from anything Alex did or said. In this case, jealousy represented the situation (time with other man), not the feeling (heartache, fear, etc.), which implies that the situation and feeling are interchangeable, marking their inevitability. The article linked Alex's jealousy to his embarrassment about her association with another man, and thus to his masculine pride. The article also assumed that they must be operating under a strictly monogamous model. The whole situation, particularly Alex's reaction, was likely fabricated, but it does represent a common story of jealousy in cultural discourse, which contributes to how people internalize feeling rules. This story must also be read in the context of gendered feeling rules, in which violence against women is frequently triggered by jealousy (Ben-Ze'ev and Goussinsky 2008).

Common in popular cultural discourse is the story of the person who feels he or she is being taken for granted by a partner. Their response is to try to make their partner feel jealous as a way to get their attention or elicit an action. For the most part, it is only in pop culture, however, that this strategy actually works. Polyamorists in my study did not interpret their partners' jealousy as a sign of love, and most abhorred the use of jealousy as a passive-aggressive tool. As Grace expressed, "I don't use jealousy as a weapon anymore." Courtney described how she was critical of conflating jealousy with a sign of love:

> Somebody can say to their lover, if you so much as look at another woman I will claw her eyes out and the person smiles because, oh that person cares. My lover cares enough about me to scratch someone's eyes out. How fucking romantic is that? That was sarcasm, little recorder.

Many participants argued that contrary to popular representations of jealousy, trying to make someone feel jealous was not a good way to spark passion or achieve a result, and they found plenty of other ways to inspire intimacy. For many people, a partner's jealousy was viewed as a barrier to their freedom to fully actualize polyamory. Coraline noted that when her partner felt jealous, her initial response was to feel guilty, as if she had done something wrong. She said it felt "toxic." For some participants, if their partner was jealous, they would curb their actions or devote more emotional energy to remedying the situation. Orion said,

> At least in my past relationships I experienced a lot of joy with my partners getting their needs met somewhere else because it frees me up a little bit. It feels really nasty and reciprocal that way but, if you go and get some ... It's more like I hope it would compel empathy or understanding in them, if you go and get some and come back and understand that it doesn't compromise our relationship, then you'll understand that I can also go out and get down with somebody else or have a relationship with somebody else and still come back to you. It's more about reciprocity than, "if you do I can."

Interestingly, Orion pointed out how having a partner participate in other relationships was comforting because other people were also taking care of her partner's needs, which consequently allowed her more space to explore other dynamics as well. One notable exception to the idea that a partner's jealousy was a barrier to intimacy was Alyson, whose partner never experienced jealousy. She wished her partner could experience it at least temporarily so she could empathize with her own challenging experiences.

Polyamorists are most likely to experience compersion when they feel as though they are being taken care of by their partners and feel secure within these relationships. Leigh explained,

> Insecurity makes poly hard … I think polyamory is very difficult. I think it's very difficult to split your energy between people. Because we are human, you have to be vastly secure to be able to do polyamory. Vastly secure in the love of the other person that they have for you and they are not going anywhere and you are not going anywhere.

Another quality useful for practising polyamory successfully is the ability to be comfortable with a degree of ambiguity. Ambiguity can sometimes induce anxiety, but polyamorists often find some stable qualities, such as the specialness of their relationship, and live with ambiguity outside of that context. This is not to say that extra-relationship sexual encounters are reasons to feel insecure or ambiguous, but such liminality is the conventional association with "affairs" and is often portrayed as triggering suspicious jealousy. Thus polyamorists must find comfort in the unknown and find security in their positions, their mutual commitment to polyamory, and, most importantly, trust. Enough trust can supersede ambiguity. Francine rarely experienced jealousy, and she connected this to her strong sense of security and secure attachment style:

> I play mind games with myself. So I take comfort in strange things that people might find really drive them to massive insecurity, where it actually makes me secure. I have my little tenets of understanding. Nobody is going to be with me unless they want to be with me. In fact the worst thing I can imagine is someone choosing to be with me out of a sense of obligation, sympathy or anything else like that. Ew. If they are with me, I have to believe they are with me because they actually want to be with me. If they stop acting like they want to be with me, I will ask them, maybe you don't want to be with me? Maybe you should move along. I have no fear of being alone. I guess that's part of it.

The issue of trust arose frequently among polyamorous participants in relation to jealousy and security in a relationship. It was particularly important to trust their partner to have responsible sex outside the relationship, both physically and emotionally. While they may know and trust their partners, they also want to be able to trust their partner's lovers, whom they may or may not know well. Uslaner (2001) categorizes approaches to trusting, two of which will be discussed here since they coincide with my participants' approaches to polyamorous practice. Moralistic trusters have an optimistic view of people, assume people are generally good, and thus are more likely to trust someone new. In the case of my participants, this would mean that a partner's choice to stay or leave is irrespective of their polyamorous practice and thus they easily trusted their partner's outside sexual and emotional actions. Strategic trusters, on the other hand, depend on accumulated information. In my research, strategic trusting polyamorists maintained scepticism and hoped to overcome distrustfulness once people proved themselves. While their core reasons for practising polyamory were strong (i.e., philosophically based or aimed towards a more realistic portrayal of their love), they had to work hard to trust the intentions of their partners and cohearts. Moralistic trusters had an easier time with compersion. Some participants straddled both sides of the fence, such as Coraline, who stated, "You trust what you know"; thus she reported that she approached her relationships not with a lack of trust but with an optimistic lack of expectations.

While expectations are shaped by socialization and culture, they are also influenced by personal history. Having a history of partners who have lied or cheated affects the likelihood of one trusting people in the future. Although polyamorous people found ways to experience sexual non-exclusivity without cheating or lying, fear of infidelity or lies may still exist. Orion admits,

> Honesty is hard. Honesty is really hard, partly because I have a nasty self-image that I'm a liar. I've been in a position of being the cheater and I'm totally aware and out and open about that because I have to be. I differentiate between the lying I did do about dating people and the way I structure my relationships now. And still don't regret any of those actions, just regret that I didn't have better communication skills and talk about my needs.

Many participants reported that honesty with themselves was the hardest aspect of relating, and once they were clear about their own expectations and intentions, honesty with their partners became less difficult. There was also a common expectation that people would disclose their polyamorous status and current lovers to any potential dates. It is no accident, therefore, that none of my participants employed a "don't ask, don't tell" policy. Notably, such a policy is practised within many open relationships.

Another strategy implemented by my participants was to meditate on loving the person connected to a jealous situation. Alex described the following:

> To convert jealousy to compersion, I focus on loving the person who is the target of my angst. For example, my first love left me for another woman. My immediate reaction was complete jealousy directed towards this "other woman," a sensation that felt a strikingly lot like hatred. My first intuition was that this anger was somehow a useful revenge, like somehow it would transform into retaliation in the form of guilt so she would not enjoy the love that she stole from me. But as you can imagine, the pain of intense jealousy was only hurting me. No revenge was had, and more importantly still, no amount of jealousy would aid my heart or win back this woman. I realized eventually that my pain was not going to mitigate the situation, and I found that the only way I was able to get over my jealousy was to convert my hate into love for this other woman. And so, for weeks I meditated on a practice of trying to love this woman. I found that it not only alleviated my jealousy but it actually became my first experience of compersion. Both of these women are still my friends to this day. I've been able to draw from this emotional toolbox and apply it to other circumstances as I've practised polyamory.

This quotation from Alex is an example of a person's ability to transform their emotions and the ability to maintain a transformed emotional state into the future. Alex was able to shift her emotional experience without shifting the circumstance that inspired her jealousy. Her lessons for inspiring compersion provided a toolbox to which she was able to return in future polyamorous experiences.

Other Challenges to Polyamory

Jealousy is not the only barrier to successful polyamory. Other common challenges include having enough time, issues regarding parenting, and maintaining safe sex practices, all of which will be addressed in brief here. The challenge of social stigma will be explored in the context of institutional power in chapter 5. Other challenges and prohibiting factors which came up during the interviews that will not be addressed here include the financial cost of dating, coming out to lovers and to the non-poly community, and meeting people to date (which may be one of the most significant challenges with dating in general).

Time

Having enough time for more than one relationship is one of the biggest barriers to polyamory. Relationships require time to sustain quality, to process dynamics, and to support one another, let alone having the mental and physical energy for multiple romances. As one participant, Priscilla, noted, "There is always room for Jell-O and always time for Facebook – and one more lover." In other words, we make time for that which we love. Just as someone may make time to watch every game of the World Series, people reshuffle their schedules and priorities when the need or want arises. Yet exactly how this is done is still mysterious.

Many polyamorists espoused the idea that quality is much more important than quantity of time spent with their partners. For example, a few hours of focused attention on each other was more valuable than many hours spent together focused on the TV in front of them, and thus they prioritized their limited time accordingly. Polyamorists find value in many forms of relationships that diverge from conventional models of relationships. For example, some polyamorists saw their lovers only once a week. Some saw their lovers, often long-distance lovers, even less often yet were able to sustain very intimate relationships. Many polyamorists talked about the difference that the "little things" make, such as short phone calls or text messages to feel connected and loved. Some polyamorists were tolerant of their partner offering them slightly less attention during the period when their partner was starting a new relationship or when an emergency in another relationship took precedence. Also of significance, when family matters or health concerns arose, polyamorists often curb the time spent in certain relationships. Another perspective, espoused by Courtney, was to have the wisdom to refrain from acting on every opportunity.

> Some people say love is infinite … but time is definitely not infinite. Sometimes you have to see a really great opportunity and just let it go by you … That was a very difficult lesson to learn. [*laughter*]

Significantly, not having enough time and energy to sustain a relationship was frequently cited as the reason relationships ended or polyamorous relationships were declined in favour of monogamous connections. A follow-up study on how time is navigated in polyamorous relationships would be particularly valuable.

Parenting

Being a parent poses many challenges to polyamorous relationships, such as the children's detachment from parental figures associated with break-ups, as well as the stigma associated with polyamory, especially as tied to dominant assumptions of model parenting. However, Sheff's (2010, 2013) research indicates that benefits of poly parenting include having more resources (material and emotional as well as role models). Parenting is a significant time commitment, making it challenging to have enough time for more than one lover. Jamieson (2004) reports that many relationships shift to monogamy when children arrive, often for temporary periods. To go out on a date means having to find someone to watch the children (if they are young) and possibly finding space outside the home for a date. When interviewing Priscilla, in the presence of her three young children, I had insight into the reality of practising poly under these circumstances. Her relationships are stifled by the chaos of daily life, the responsibilities of parenthood, and the limits of time, but she also knew the strength of parental love, a quality highly relevant to loving multiple people and juggling multiple relationships. She also had several people in her poly family who had parental roles for her children, comparable to aunts and uncles. Notably, she was not actively polyamorous during the first few years of her children's life, even though her wife was actively polyamorous, but she started dating again once they were old enough to be watched over by other childcare providers. Similarly, Heloise remarked on how being a parent to a second child offered insight into loving multiple people:

> I felt this sadness when my wife was pregnant with our second child, because I was like, there is no way we are going to be able to love a second child the same way because there is no way we can feel this [much love]. There is no room for me to feel this about another person. And then you do … So yeah, of course you can be poly. Yes, I can be this in love with two people.

Notably, equating loving multiple children with the compersive ability to love multiple people should not imply that all parental love is virtuous.

Parents can be aggressive and possessive in ways that are akin to jealousy. Parents have also been known to give preference to one child over others, to be jealous of their children, or to provoke competition between siblings.

Another participant had a poly rule wherein if she or her husband went out on a date with a secondary lover, this lover would have to spend another evening watching her two young children. She reasoned that if the lover took time away from the family, they must also return time to the family. She reported an unintended benefit of this structure: the children gained multiple adult role models. Heloise was very open with her children about her polyamorous practice and would introduce her children to her partners because she said, "I do not want to model to my children a monogamous paradigm. I want my children to grow up having poly be a part of their lives." However, she did not introduce a partner into the family until she was clear that this person would become a part of their life for the long term, whether as a friend or a lover. Heloise also emphasized the importance of seeing affection and joy in adult role models and fondly remembered witnessing affection between her loving parents.

There was also the challenge of introducing the children to a new lover. The opinion and practice of the participants varied regarding if and when this was done. Cheyenne lived with her family of three lovers (of fluctuating friend/lover status) and her child was fully aware of these relationships. She was comfortable interacting with them all together, and while she would not do anything overtly sexual in the presence of the children, she would be affectionate. The child would sometimes talk about his two mothers and two fathers and in other situations would talk about his mother, father, and their roommates. This shift in his expression of their relationship titles depended on his comfort in given situations and demonstrated his agency in the situation. His mother reported having full respect for his control over disclosure. Children often do not know families are different until they are told as much, and because he grew up in a poly household, he had normalized having a large, loving, non-nuclear family.

Cheyenne talked about her fear that her child would grow up confusing friends with lovers and with family. She argued that because adult relationships are complex and he only saw glimpses of the dynamics, which are interpreted through a child's lens, he may not understand. Therefore, she let him ask questions at his own pace. Heloise described the benefits of her child seeing love and affection in many forms, particularly growing up in a loving household and environment. This participant noted that although the nuclear family is normalized in Western culture, it is far from the most common familial structure. Tianna hid her polyamorous relationships from her son while he was a child, but once he became a teenager, she realized that he had been fully aware of her polyamorous practice throughout his upbringing and was relatively comfortable with it. There is a significant cultural assumption that the heterosexual, nuclear family is the superior environment in which to raise a family, and therefore alternative family structures tend to be under greater and disproportionate scrutiny. Further research on children who grew up in non-monogamous households would be very valuable.

Safer Sex

Safer sex was at once very important to my participants and not very challenging to accomplish. Many polyamorists practised safer sex (barriers, gloves, condoms, etc.) with their lovers. Some were "fluid bonded" (i.e., they deliberately have non-barrier sex) with only one person (often their primary) and used barriers with all other lovers. The upfront clarity about sexual practices placed polyamorous people at a lesser risk than some other groups (particularly people who cheat and those who are "dating around"). In the earlier example where a participant was in a chain of lovers and one had a manageable sexually transmitted infection (STI), the doctor informed her that she was in a very low-risk group because of the openness of communication and the respect/desire for the infection not to be transmitted. According to the doctor in this scenario, people are at more risk when STIs are unknown, people are unwilling to disclose, or their sexual partners are anonymous. Polyamorists pride themselves on their open communication about sexuality and about full disclosure of all people with whom they are involved sexually. At least in theory. In a previous example, I discussed the "ultimate poly betrayal," where a woman found out her partner was having unsafe sex with a known lover. (Luckily, no STIs were transmitted in this circumstance, but the relationship ended.) Notably, lesbians are often considered to be in a lower-risk group for many major STIs, and this fact is relevant to the observations.

Compersion and the Benefits of Polyamory

The polyagonous narratives shared so far may lead one to ask why polyamorists continue to practise polyamory through such difficult emotions. My research indicates that the answer is manifold. First, while jealousy in polyamory can be difficult, there is jealousy in monogamous practice as well. Second, once tools are in place to manage difficult emotions such as jealousy, it is experienced less negatively. Most polyamorists stated that jealousy was more common in their early experiences of polyamory and became increasingly rarer. Third, the tools in place to mitigate jealousy in polyamorists' relationships could be applied to other difficult emotions. Fourth, my participants described polyamory as a much more realistic and freeing expression of their love and sexuality than monogamy would be and thus welcomed the full package. They see polyamory as no less normal than monogamy, just less common. Several participants talked about being able to love every partner more when they did not feel confined by a monogamous model. For example, Cheyenne stated,

> I'm still attracted to every second person who walks down the street! I have a lot of attractions and I find a lot of people attractive and I really enjoy having crushes, even if that's all that they are. I just love that energy and I find any kind of school environment or work environment more interesting if there's someone you have a crush on in the milieu. I don't feel my own attractions to people diminish in this relationship. I just feel more careful about how that's expressed or how much I really pursue.

Fifth, the benefits of polyamory outweigh the difficult feelings, and the pleasure found in compersion is particularly satisfying. Martha noted the opportunities for healing and passion from having multiple lovers: "I really believe in the powerful healing effects of sex. And not just in sexual ways, not just around sexual issues ... I just feel more alive." Sixth, the challenge of polyamory and its ensuing opportunity for growth was highly gratifying. And last, sexual enjoyment was a significant benefit of polyamorous practice. Indeed, consider this polyamorous joke: What is the plural of spouse? Spice.

Studies have shown that open relationships correlate to increased self-esteem and self-knowledge (Wolfe 2008), personal empowerment and independence (Cardoso et al. 2009; Sheff 2005; Weitzman 1999; Wilkins 2004), and "boosts in sexual self-confidence ... and [the] dissolution of jealousy" (De Visser and McDonald 2007, 469). My study reveals similar results. Martha stated, "I encounter different people and they bring out different parts of me ... I feel like engaging with multiple people helps me understand the fullness of me." Similarly, Cheyenne talked about polyamory as empowering and felt a great deal of pride and satisfaction in bringing her jealousy to a place of solid compersion:

> You know those moments when you feel really proud of yourself about the way you live and what you do. Like, "Look at us!" And I do, I feel so attached to that word [compersion], really excited that I do receive so much pleasure from my partner being off with someone else and having a great night. I want to hear about it the next day in whatever degree of detail they want to give me. And that's fun.

Another participant, Nora, responded,

> It is all worthwhile for me to do it. It's a beautiful thing. It's like getting your cake and eating it too. Even if it means the making of the cake is six times longer, it's worth it. It's the most difficult cake in the universe to make.

Although many polyamorists maintain "It's not all about the sex,"[14] the sexual benefits of polyamory were frequently mentioned in the interviews. Several polyamorists talked about eroticizing what may have otherwise triggered jealousy (such as a partner having sex with someone else), thus converting a potentially painful event into one of arousal. Research on swinging has also demonstrated that certain situations which are typically ripe for jealousy had an erotically stimulating effect on swingers (De Visser and McDonald 2007; Gould 1999). Similarly, Stearns (1989, 15) notes that a certain amount of jealousy can "provide some enjoyable spice." Many polyamorists reported that having outside sexual experiences increased their overall libido and that this increase is transferred to their other partners. When thinking about a hypothetical situation that would make her jealous, Heloise said it made her feel "sad. Sad and then hot. Like a good hot, but a flush of woah!" Similarly, Courtney expressed a strong sense of sexual compersion:

> I'm so compersive, it's painful. Literally, it's like blue balls ... If my lover has a lover who I am friends with or who I like, and this is about 98% of the time, watching them hug, kiss, snuggle, love, have sex with that person, is so hot I could almost die from it. It's not even a vague pleasure. It's like, oh my God, right. It's the hottest thing ever. Ever. And the better I like the person that my lover is having sex with, the hotter it is.

---

14   This phrase was popularized by the podcast *PolyWeekly* by Cunning Minx.

Orion described an experience of sexual compersion as well:

> We had a hot make-out which was punctuated with dirty talk about other lovers. She was like, "tell me a nasty story about you getting down with so and so." And our interaction was framed by hotness coming from somewhere else.

Another account of sexual compersion came from Martha:

> The thought of someone fucking my partner in front of me, like I really get off on that. Maybe it's just the fact that I'm very open and I like the idea of group sex and I like the idea of watching. And that just gets me off, so I think I would have a sense of compersion watching my partner being pleasured by somebody else.

Heloise described another aspect of compersion, regarding how outside sexual encounters rekindled connectivity, spark, and appreciation within her primary relationship:

> It's funny because if you look at the [article in a magazine on] "How do you know if your spouse is cheating?" and some of the big signs are, he's suddenly bringing you gifts, they're telling you they love you more, and you are having more sex. And I'm like "Right, what's wrong with that?" Okay, so find out who they are cheating with so they stop doing all those wonderful things for you. I mean the concept is that they are doing it out of guilt, but it could be that they are feeling more sexual and more loving and more gregarious.

Dominique explained that if she were to go out on a date with a secondary partner, she would have to arrange a special date with her primary, and this was part of how they kept the spark alive in their relationship, which was going on nine years. In these examples, we can see not solely a transformation of jealousy to compersion but also an unintended benefit of the sexual arousal and general spark within the other relationship(s).

Conclusion

Love's shadow is jealousy – and jealousy plays a significant role in the polyamorous experience, through either its presence or its absence. It may be that the more people open their hearts to truly open relationships, the more vulnerable they are to the experience of jealousy or, alternatively, the more they can conquer love's shadow. Through their extensive critique and re-imagining of jealousy, polyamorists seek to shift personal and cultural understandings of jealousy. Compersion is a creative act of resistance that places the body, pleasure, and love at centre stage. Polyamorists' practice of compersion challenges emotionally normative constructions of jealousy.

The creation of the word "compersion," arguably, has contributed to the potential for it to be experienced. When experience is bound by particular feeling rules, it can be difficult to experience emotional outcomes outside of this box. If, for example, one assumes love must be directed towards only one person, then any attraction to a third party may be interpreted as a failure of love, or possibly evidence that the prior love was illegitimate. But as many people who have been in long-term relationships can attest, such criterion sets up nearly impossible parameters, and these can actually interfere with the value of the relationship. Polyamorists vie for their own parameters and thus try to live up to the standards they create. The cultivation of their experience, both sexual and emotional, through the development of language and culture can shift emotional outcomes.

From the interviews I conducted, I found that my participants (usually) experienced more polyamory than polyagony. It could be that those who struggled greatly are no longer polyamorous and therefore did not make it into my sample. My sample represents people who have enough social and cultural capital as well as education to be able to persevere with polyamory, which then must also influence their approach to processing jealousy. My data suggests that jealousy is manageable for many polyamorists, as long as all practitioners are willing to reflect and do the work. The experience of polyamory contradicts conventional beliefs about the naturalness and inevitability of jealousy and the supposed gendered ways that jealousy is embodied. While polyamorists do not necessarily have different emotional experiences than monogamous people, they follow a different model of love that in turn affects their emotional experience. Through the creation of a cultural ideology of poly, polyamorists intend to cultivate the emotional experience of compersion. Polyamory exemplifies a culture where sexual non-exclusivity and jealousy are not necessarily associated and offers an alternative narrative of the embodiment and expression of jealousy.

4 Once You Say, "I'm Poly," It Kind of Eliminates the Need for the Feminist Part: Gender, Jealousy, and Polyamory

The most radical thing we can do as feminists is to treat our happy, open, free lives as if they were simply normal.

Courtney (study participant)

Gender plays an intricate role in romantic relationships and is part of how people relate to each other sexually. Gender means more than the categories of man and woman; it extends to the matrices of ways in which people relate to their identities, roles, and expressions of masculinity and femininity, and to their distance from these categories. Understandings of one's gendered subjectivity are also tied to emotional experiences, particularly emotions that are connected to sexuality, the body, and intimate interactions. It is nearly impossible to separate emotion from the constructs of gender, sexuality, and their intersecting regulation. In refusing to participate in compulsory monogamy, do polyamorous queer women also resist heteronormativity, genderism, sexism, and emotional normativity? While creating new relationship structures and emotional dynamics, does this population also play with, re-imagine, and transform the gendered feeling rules of jealousy, sexuality, and the body? Barbalet (1998, 180) notes that "emotions are never in fact 'finished projects' but always in process." Although emotions are always in flux, I look at an illustrative moment of polyamorous discourse to see how the intersection of gender and jealousy is re-imagined by my sample of polyamorous queer women. I found that their resistance to gendered feeling rules was contextual – at times successful and at other times reproducing the very structures they intended to resist.

Emotional norms are repeatedly reinforced in social interactions. As mentioned previously, the fact that there is no word for the opposite of jealousy in the English language (prior to the coinage of "compersion") reveals a key feeling rule in Western culture – i.e., that jealousy is the expected reaction to a lover's affection towards another person. Expressing socially unacceptable (or "inappropriate") emotions tends to be met with scorn, shame, or ridicule. By experiencing pleasure where others proclaim they ought to feel jealousy, polyamorists might be considered "emotional deviants" (Thoits 2012) since they violate conventions of emotional norms. Lupton (1998, 84) notes,

> The notion that the emotions are disruptive and somehow external to the self remains dominant in contemporary Western societies. Indeed, we commonly talk about the emotions in terms that suggest that we are passive and even helpless in the face of the power of emotions, suggesting that we often find ourselves submitting to them or over-powered by them despite our better judgment or our best efforts.

Part of the intention of the polyamorist movement is to rebuild emotional and social models of relationships, not as passive servants of emotions but as active creators of their emotional world. The self, after all, cannot be distinguished from our emotional lives. People shape and are shaped by affect. For many polyamorous queer women in my sample, practising compersion was seen as an act of resistance to conventional discourses on emotion, sexuality, gender, and relationship structures. The active pursuit of the emotional pleasure of compersion, particularly embodied pleasure, was often understood by these polyamorists as a feminist practice in itself. This act was seen as a form of resistance to the dominant discourse, in which jealousy is the only legitimate response to a lover's affection for another person.

Representations both in the media and in research reinforce the gender dichotomy which states that men and women are triggered by, experience, and express jealousy differently. A brief summary of the typical gender divide is that women are more inclined to experience jealousy when their partner has an emotional connection (real or imagined) to another person, while men are apparently more likely to experience jealousy when their lover has a sexual connection with another person (Buss 2000). There is also literature that claims women respond to jealousy-inducing situations with cattiness and manipulative behaviour or by working on the relationship, whereas men respond with anger, aggression, and violence (Clanton 1996). Jealousy has been linked to sexual and material property in marriage, the regulation of sexuality, competition, male violence, and paternal lineage (Clanton and Smith 1977; White and Mullen 1989), all of which are connected to constructions of gender. Representations of gender roles and emotional norms contribute to the embodiment of jealousy, and thus the gender divide becomes self-fulfilling. As Petersen (2004, 53) argues, "by learning the culturally prescribed feeling rules for those of their gender, men and women are socialized into different emotional worlds."

There is some validity to gendered stereotypes; some people easily embody society's gender ideal and other people work very hard to fit it. Most people, however, fit somewhere within a matrix of patterns and traits associated with masculinity and femininity that shift with time and context. Social ideas contribute to embodied feelings. Emotional norms are repeatedly reinforced through social interactions until they seem "natural" and are interpreted as "fact," similar to the way gender is constructed through repetition (Butler 1990). My analysis of queer women's polyamory contributes to a critical analysis of the social context of jealousy. While looking at how social ideas are transformed into feelings and how feelings are transformed into social ideas, I also examine how such ideas and consequently their embodiment can shift.

The categories of man and woman are social constructs with "fuzzy" parameters (Tauchert 2002), but gender occupies real space in the everyday lives of individuals, whether through the replication of categories or through the continuous displacement of these categories (Butler 1990). In other words, even those individuals who embody gender-queer existence and who challenge the categories are often confronted with the reification of gender. Thus, while I challenge the gender binary, I remain aware of the importance of these categories to my participants and to the contemporary spaces in which gender is lived.

In my analysis of the interview data, I found evidence that demonstrates stereotypical gendered patterns, but I also found a wide range of stories that point to the vast diversity of emotional experiences. My research on queer women's polyamory demonstrates the limitations of dichotomizing emotional experiences by gender, and it also makes evident the intricate connection between socialized gender discourse and emotional experiences. I address the intersection of gender and jealousy in polyamory by looking at my sample of polyamorous queer women's perspectives regarding feminism, promiscuity, competition between women, and emotional control.

My research shows that the polyamorous queer women in my sample are re-imagining the gendered connection between love and relationships. They challenge many of the ideas entrenched in monogamy – such as the idea that sexual exclusivity is the only way to express love and commitment – and they replace these with alternative values. In particular, they state that jealousy is neither inevitable nor intolerable, nor is it necessarily tied to fixed gendered roles. Instead one can experience jealousy, navigate it, and move past the negative emotion to a positive one (i.e., compersion). In this way, polyamorous queer women attempt to rewrite the gendered feeling rules regarding jealousy. They do so by constructing new norms, ideas, and guidelines that steer their practice as a culture, making compersion not only possible but common. These norms inform how they structure emotional experiences, actualize gender equality, and strengthen their personal sense of sexual freedom. As many marginalized populations have done, polyamorists both resist dominant structures that regulate emotion, gender, and sexuality (which are highly intertwined) and create alternatives that suit their preferences. However, like most cultural norms, these are not always followed; they are always in flux, and the norms in place to mitigate jealousy and minimize sexism do not work for everybody. As well, the patriarchal and mono-normative society in which we live, and out of which polyamory emerged, requires more than a discursive deconstruction to be adequately rewired.

Polyamory as a Feminist Practice

Polyamory is often described as having a feminist framework (Mint 2007a) since many prominent polyamory advocates are feminist (Barker 2005; Easton and Liszt 1997; Haritaworn, Lin, and Klesse 2006; Sheff 2006; Taormino 2008). Indeed, polyamory's pronounced emphasis on gender equality is one of the features that distinguishes it from other forms of non-monogamy, such as free love, swinging, or polygamy. Feminism and polyamory share a critique of institutionalized monogamy (Barker and Ritchie 2007; Overall 1998; Robinson 1997), as well as a political and social analysis of sexuality (Easton and Liszt 1997; Ritchie and Barker 2006). According to Barker and Ritchie (2007), polyamory is not only culturally feminist but also women-centred since many of the skills required for polyamory to function smoothly, such as managing relationships and emotional communication, are skills at which women stereotypically excel. While this can valorize women's position in the poly community, it can also mean that women are nudged into conventional roles or are burdened with a greater workload in the gendered division of labour.

According to Boler (1999, 109),

> The "feminist politics of emotion" is a theory and practice that invites women to articulate and publicly name their emotions, and to critically and collectively analyse these emotions not as "natural," "private" occurrences but rather as reflecting learned hierarchies and gendered roles. The feminist practices of consciousness-raising and feminist pedagogy powerfully reclaim emotions out of the (patriarchally enforced) private sphere and put emotions on the political and public map. Feminist politics of emotion recognize emotions not only as a site of social control, but of political resistance.

Polyamorous discourse reflects Boler's statement in that it critiques the alleged naturalness and gendered aspects of jealousy. A common polyamorous critique of the institution of monogamy points to the way jealousy functions as a mechanism of social control (Klesse 2006b), and thus polyamorous practice constitutes political resistance through the embodied manifestation of compersion. Although the feminist leaning of the polyamorous movement is well articulated, the range of meaning given to feminism and the ways in which it plays out in polyamorous practice vary significantly. The dynamics of feminist practice in polyamory and the feminist politics of emotion (as identified by Boler 1999) are explored in this section.

Many of my participants viewed their polyamorous practice as necessarily feminist. Their understandings of feminism varied, but many strongly believed in the connection between their choice to practise polyamory and the values of self-determination, non-possessiveness, gender equality, and sexual freedom. Here are a few examples:

> I don't even have to say feminist anymore since I've been poly and dating people. It seems like once you say, "I'm poly," then it kind of eliminates the need for the feminist part. (Brianna)
>
> My poly wasn't externally informed, it was internally informed. So, it's not that I've chosen poly out of a particular political statement. My political statement supports poly because feminism is ultimately about self-determination for women. In a nutshell. And poly for me is about a self-determinationist expression of my sexuality. (Coraline)
>
> That's what feminism means to me, fighting against the oppression that limits people's choices and their ability of self-expression and for living

their lives … Any relationship can be oppressive, poly or not. So to me, it's about building relationships where each person in that relationship has their voice and is honoured and respected and is able to grow as a person. (Cheyenne)

Everything I do is connected to my choices about feminism and living life not just as a making me happy thing, but also as an open political statement. The most radical thing we can do as feminists is to treat our happy, open, free lives as if they were simply normal. I am not in rebellion against anything because to do so simply redefines the status quo as quo status. I live my own life in a perfectly normal happy way and that it doesn't happen to match many other people's lives is their loss entirely. (Courtney)

Courtney equated the pursuit of happiness with a political action. For many of my participants, being feminist influenced their choice of with whom they would develop a relationship. Alex explained that she would only date people who identified as feminists. She reasoned that being in a polyamorous dynamic required people to be able to take care of and strongly vocalize their needs, which were qualities that defined her feminist choices. In regard to her feminism, Alasia stated,

I don't think I've ever slept with a woman that I found out wasn't feminist. And I've grown pretty aware of how I like feminist lovers, male or female. But whether it has to do with poly or not? Maybe part of it, besides the honesty that I would rather not cheat, and that we don't own each other. And if a person is doing something that gives them joy, gives somebody else joy, it seems a pinched attitude to prevent them from doing that based on some ownership issues. Mainly like "you belong to me."

Alasia's statement highlights the polyamorous value of non-possessiveness which comes out of the critique of monogamy as a form of ownership.

Discussion of non-monogamy has persisted in different streams of feminist thought, with a variety of emphases, challenges, and critiques. These variations in approaches to polyamory were apparent in my sample. Alasia evoked the socialist feminist argument that non-monogamy was a political extension of the critique of capitalism, since the patriarchal institution of marriage benefits men through control of women's reproduction, sexuality, and domestic services, as well as diverting all of one's emotional and political energy into one's "other half." Coraline discussed how 25 years ago in her queer community, it was completely unacceptable in that time period to actually be poly … And I was pretty closeted. I lived in a lesbian feminist collective household and really could not talk about my experience of wanting to be poly without having a huge amount of judgment.

Whereas Coraline continued to identify as a feminist despite the tension between her desire and the political atmosphere in which she lived, Alyson was more conflicted about her identification as a feminist:

I used to be [a feminist], but I'm not sure what it means anymore or if I am included in the equation, so I don't know … It was also my experience coming out in the 80s as a feminist, as a lesbian and then the whole Sex Wars thing erupted and I have never reconciled how do you be sex-positive and be a feminist and be a genderqueer? So on a day-to-day level I certainly fight for those things but the word feminist in itself now feels like a box and I am on the outside of that box.

Polyamory emerged in part as a response to the free love movement and its separation of sex and love (Zell [1990] 2014). The free love movement of the 1960s emerged in resistance to limiting norms of compulsory monogamy, premarital sex, and general sexual taboos. As free love followers broke out of conservative norms, they swung to the other end of the spectrum, disconnecting sexuality from commitments and from emotional intimacy. Whereas polyamory retains the celebration of sexual connections with multiple people, it contrasts the free love movement by re-establishing a strong connection among sexual acts, commitment, and emotional intimacy. Polyamory also benefits from decades of development of feminist thought. Two of my participants described how their mothers participated in the free love movement and saw open relationships as solely benefiting men because the boyfriends of their youth would tout emotional non-attachment to sex and use this to justify their promiscuity and lack of relationship accountability. Heloise described this sentiment as, "it's just sex. It means nothing." However, their boyfriends would not tolerate their enjoyment of sexual encounters outside of the relationship. Heloise told this story:

A lot of my family comes out of the 60s, which is great in many ways, but the whole poly/non-monogamy of the 60s was very different, which tended to be that the men got to sleep around and the women didn't. My mother's experience was just that. My father got to sleep with other people and the couple of times she did, he hit the roof and went ballistic. So that is the model of non-monogamy that she had, so she found the idea of me being non-monogamous stressful.

Rihanna came of age during the 1960s and noted that from her perspective,

the other misconception of polyamory is that it's all for the men and it never works for women … that it's the guy who is getting the most benefit out of it.

Similarly, Brianna, who was active in the bisexual community, noted that many people still assumed that men were the main beneficiaries of polyamory:

It's funny because often times when I try to explain it, there is a moment when the person I'm talking to goes, "oh, so the women are allowed to have partners too?" That's like, ah, wow, yeah. Do I seem like the kind of woman who would agree to anything else?

In spite of the fact that many of the women in my sample identified as feminists and deliberately challenged gender rules, conventional gender stereotypes still endured, albeit in an altered form reflective of their queer culture. There was a subtle reproduction of the virgin/whore dichotomy dividing the "good" partner from the "promiscuous" partner, reminiscent of the double standard in heterosexual non-monogamy. For example, Nora described a polyamorous couple she knew and how she felt bad for the partner who she perceived as staying at home with the kids while her wife "gallivanted" around town on her many dates. Dominique said that people in her community, including polyamorists, looked at her with pity in response to the seeming promiscuity of her partner.

Because I'm less active in it, and even when I'm active people don't always know about it because I'm a more private person, I don't always let people know what I'm doing. People often come to me and do this, you'll love this: [*look of dreadful pity*] "How's it going with Leigh? Are you alright?" I hate that. When they go on with that shit, that bugs my ass … Pity, yeah, and digging around for stories, like drama … Yeah, they perceived [that I have] no power, even though for nine years, I came into this when you had a partner and we stayed. People don't look at that. People look at the other stuff ... I always say, I'm really careful ... I do this voluntarily. This is consensual, we talk, Leigh is really responsible. If she has a date with [her coheart] or someone, then she has a really big date with me.

In Dominique's case, there was a strong butch-femme dynamic, and the butch/masculine partner was perceived as being more active, which exacerbated people's perception of a power imbalance between the couple along conventional gender lines. It appears that people still unconsciously buy into gender roles about appropriate behaviour for men and women, where a butch person is cast in the man's role. Some polyamorists appear to be harder on masculine people when they appear to replicate male promiscuity. By pitying Dominique and digging for stories, people were casting her in a traditional female role, in which women are argued to be more susceptible to gossip in connection to jealousy and envy. This pity is also tied into assumptions about jealousy; the assumption is that the one who is more active has more power and hence the less active partner will be more susceptible to jealousy.

Alyson also noted how people felt sorry for her when she was partnered with someone who actively self-identified as "trampy":

Well when I went out with [her] and I tried to explain it to people, people just felt sorry for me and it's just like, you know what? I don't need this. I've never come up with a different way, clearly I was delivering the message poorly, but I don't know how you convey that to people and have that just be okay, this is how it is.

As illustrated in the quotes from Dominique and Alyson, some polyamorists embraced discrepancies that could be considered a "double standard" in relation to activity or quantity of partners. In other words, far from being pitied, polyamorists found it okay for one person to be dating more people than the other. The goal is not to equalize power by imposing the same rules or same numbers on all parties, but rather to focus on consent, mutual satisfaction, and meeting individual needs. That said, many of my participants found their jealousy more easily navigated when they were the person who dated more. For example, Orion described how being the partner who was more active coincided with her experiencing less jealousy in the relationship.

I haven't lately been the person who experienced jealousy ... because I have a tendency to be the really slutty one. At least in my past relationships

I experienced a lot of joy with my partners getting their needs met some-where else because it frees me up a little bit.

Similarly to Orion, Courtney described how it felt to be the one who tended to be more active and how she would take the brunt of the criticism:

I find it fascinating that most of the stuff around poly support goes along the lines of how the sluttier of the two partners should be very supportive to their less slutty partner. And it's very common and stern that they say you should go no faster than your partner can deal with. That you should be very careful, be very understanding. The fact that your partner spent the last 3 hours yelling that Krissy is a bitch and a slut and a whore and that she's ugly and she's got spots and her hair is badly styled and she doesn't know what you see in her. That you should be patient because that is actually your partner's way of saying, I feel frightened now and I need reassurance. [*laughter*] And it's also common for people who are marginally poly or who are not poly at all to speak to you when you talk about your poly problems as if it were entirely your fault for being trampy. If you loved her enough though, couldn't you just dump that other person? If you really cared about her though, wouldn't you want to be with her and nobody else? Right? So I find that there are very few resources out there for the trampiest of poly people, who just want to be in a relationship and love someone and also love someone else.

Courtney's comment brings to light a dissonance between polyam-orous beliefs and behaviours. Whereas most polyamorous discourse is sympathetic to the partner who is experiencing jealousy, the dis-course rarely addresses the challenges of being the more active part-ner or being the person towards whom this jealousy is directed. She points out that it is also emotionally challenging to be the partner of someone experiencing jealousy in response to your consensual behav-iour. Her statement also makes apparent the social stigma regarding polyamory's connection to "sluttiness," which is faced, and at times reproduced, by polyamorists. In this instance, the assumption con-tinues to be that if a person loved her partner enough, she would not need to seek the romantic/sexual attention of others. In polyamorous culture, there is a complicated reclamation of the word "slut." After all, the "bible of polyamory" is called *The Ethical Slut,* named so to call attention to the assumption that non-monogamy is an act of promiscuity, and hence taking back its power, much like the reclamation of "queer." The authors describe their reclamation as follows:

> We are proud to reclaim the word "slut" as a term of approval, even endearment. To us, a slut is a person of any gender who has the courage to lead life according to the radical proposition that *sex is nice and pleasure is good for you.* (Easton and Liszt 1997, 4; emphasis in original)

Mint (2008, 22), a popular online blogger, believes that "the poly movement needs slut pride." He argues that in an attempt to gain mainstream credibility, polyamorists have downplayed the sexual component of polyamory while emphasizing the love aspect. One example of this is the often-used comparison of a polyamorist to a parent who loves more than one child. While this strategy has been somewhat successful, it masks the reality of what draws people to polyamory and what makes such relationships different – i.e., the sex. As Mint (2008, 24) argues, "the urge to hide these aspects of polyamory is counterproductive to our movement: in particular, it makes for crappy advertising." Also, such a strategy replicates the sex-negativity of the dominant culture. Minimizing or masking the sexual component of polyamory leads to the problem of judgment, dividing the good from the bad partner of the polyamorous unit. By unapologetically embracing the sexual component of polyamory, Mint (2008) argues that polyamorists will more successfully challenge sex-negative assumptions in mono-normative culture.

In the following quotation, Ren described how she had internalized a sense of shame in her desire to have more than one lover and how polyamory helped her overcome the negativity she associated with promiscuity. She had internalized the monogamous assumption that

> because I loved her and I felt like I should be okay with being monogamous [even though I] was unhappy for a chunk of that relationship [and] was ashamed because I knew I had these major desires ... I should not want to slut it up. So I think it silenced me. But I saw how destructive it was, how I lost so many parts of myself. So now I try to be really conscious that if I ever do feel ashamed to really look at it and pull it away from me and see that again it's about oppression of people and silencing of love.

Ren's polyamorous and feminist choices, as well as participation in the community in which these ideas took shape, helped her overcome the shame she felt regarding her sexual desire. Ren described polyamory as an expression of self-love and acts of pleasure as an important route in her personal reclamation of "slut pride." She stated,

> If people are loved and confident then they will start revolutions ... And by love, I mean self-love, ultimately, the most. That's the biggest. Like all of these relationships, my relationship with myself is the only one I can guarantee ... I think it's a symbiotic relationship where I reflect back at you and you reflect back at me and we can both learn and grow and celebrate each other. If I try to hold on to something I'm just going to kill it. If I'm celebrating and supporting its life, then it's going to grow and I'm going to grow and we are going to both benefit. Magic!

This reclamation of the slut is not synonymous with "anything goes." My participants were critical of any pressure to have more lovers than they wanted. Cheyenne used the term "poly at all costs" to refer to polyamorists who felt they needed to have multiple partners regardless of the circumstances. My participants often looked down on this idea and found it more balanced to pick and choose when and with whom to engage in relationships, taking a break when their offspring were young, for example, or when a family emergency arose. Cheyenne noted,

> There were times when we focused in or when we were struggling and not communicating well or not meeting each other well and then we can't be going off with other people if we are not feeling safe or feeling like we are doing this well on our own terms. And I really respect that ebb and flow. If it's all poly all the time, poly at all costs then you are not necessarily, in my experience, not listening to myself or listening to my partner. And I think you can be committed to living your life that way, but not all the time ... That's the whole point.

At the same time, the needs of one part of a poly configuration should be balanced with the needs of and respect for secondary lovers. A feminist politics of emotion works to challenge the shame connected with norms of sexuality and compulsory monogamy, but not through the imposition of new boxes. The feminist intentions of polyamorists are to develop ethical, egalitarian relationships with sex-positive attitudes as well as the emotional experience of compersion.

Cohearts and Competition between Women

I'm sexy. I'm pretty. I look great in a pair of stilettos and I can work it.

Tianna (study participant)

Jealousy's connection to the gender of one's coheart can be traced to socialized competition between women (Barash 2006). Barash suggests that women are more likely to compete with other women colleagues than with their male colleagues. Similarly, women are socialized to compete with other women in regard to beauty, and the result comes out as envy, gossip, or scorn directed at the ones considered more beautiful among them (Tanenbaum 2000; Wolfe 1992). Ben-Ze'ev and Goussinsky (2008, 208) argue,

> It has been shown that jealousy increases when the rival's qualities pertain to a domain relevant to one's self-esteem. Thus, individuals who attribute great importance to physical attractiveness are more likely to demonstrate a jealous reaction if their rival is unusually attractive.

This competition played out among many polyamorists in my study who experienced jealousy when they perceived their coheart to be more beautiful than they considered themselves to be. Tianna noted,

> I'm jealous about the other person, like if she's prettier or smarter, or funnier, like it's more of a personal comparison … Yeah, there was this one girl that she went on a date with that I didn't think was very hot. I looked at her and was like, hmm, no, whatever. But apparently everybody in the whole world thinks this girl is a total knockout … Sometimes I'll remind myself of my good qualities, like with the girl where I felt that little twinge of jealousy, I just told myself she's not all that. I'm pretty hot myself, not to be egotistical but you know, I'm sexy. I'm pretty. I look great in a pair of stilettos and I can work it.

In this example, Tianna replicated the conventional gender norm of beauty and attractiveness as the defining measure of one's worth and of one's place in the competition. Similarly, Heloise described feeling jealous in regard to comparisons with her coheart's physical traits: "They are high femme and I am not high femme. They are thin and I know that is a value to her sexually. And they are younger than me." Brianna overcame her sense of competition regarding the beauty of her coheart in the following way:

> At the beginning I was always worried about looks. I was feeling insecure about that for some reason. But then I realized that we really wanted to be in a triad so then it became about them finding the best looking partner so I would be attracted to them. Best looking to me, but that hasn't really worked out because he has different taste than I do.

My participants often compared their experience of jealousy to tropes represented in dominant culture. Many portrayals of jealousy in the media, for example, rely on the archetype of the rival, such as two women competing for the attention of a man, the "other woman" intruding on a couple and "breaking them up."[15] Cheyenne described the way messages of jealousy are constructed:

> Because there are all the messages around us saying that if your partner were to be with someone else that would be a devastating thing and you should be jealous about that, not even being with someone else but finding someone else attractive, then you should be jealous about it.

Although dominant portrayals do not accurately represent relationships, these stories do contribute to people's understanding of emotion and to the ways in which emotion is embodied. Gendered feeling rules are social ideas that are never statically embodied. As Butler (1990) notes, gender needs to be continuously reinforced through repetition for it to take on a semblance of a reified position. Socialization has an impact on people's understanding of feeling rules, as well as on what one actually does feel. The norms that reinforce competition between women are made apparent through regulatory bodies and the means by which emotions are learned – including media, mono-normativity, genderism, heterosexism, sexism, etc. Competition between women in the polyamorous community is often based in, or portrayed as a site of,

---

15   For example, Avril Lavigne's music video for "Girlfriend" is a retelling of this classic tale, and it is a frequently viewed video on YouTube.

potential jealousy. Such competition is actively critiqued by polyamorists, but at times it is also replicated in the subculture.

Many of my participants reported a connection between the gender of one's coheart and the way they experienced jealousy related to competition. For example, Alex, who identified as butch, noted how it was easier when her femme lover dated people who were not butches. People who reminded her of herself in terms of gender were more likely to inspire jealousy. This also applied to people who were similar to her in terms of other traits, including being a sexual top, older than her lover, or aesthetically similar. Martha offered an example of how her partner would feel jealous in regard to one of her core insecurities, that she is uninteresting: "If I have connections with other people then I will realize how boring she is."

Many people are less likely to feel jealous of a person who is vastly different or removed from themselves, since they are seen as complementary rather than as competition. Grace's partner was a female-to-male transgendered person, and she said, "He's often jealous of people with a more masculine gender presentation, or sometimes lately a genderqueer presentation. It's the gender thing that gets him going." On the other hand, she found it more challenging when her coheart was differently gendered. Grace said,

> I used to be really jealous when he would date men, specifically biological men. As opposed to the similar gender presentation thing it was the polar opposite, like this person can give you something that I can't or I feel like I can't … If he is dating men I like to meet them because I find that whole male-male relationship rather threatening because I feel so excluded from it … With the guy situation, I don't get jealous if I know them or I definitely get less jealous if I know them because they're never as threatening and beautiful and big bulky boy as I think they'll be before I meet them. Which really threatens me, or has in the past and I just get that meeting out of the way so it doesn't have a chance to develop there.

Among my bisexual participants, jealousy regarding the gender of the coheart took another twist. For example, Brianna noted how her boyfriend at times exhibited the stereotypical male response to her other lovers, in which he minimized her relationships with women:

> He's internalized a little of the heteronormative stuff in that he is more comfortable if I am dating women, but he fully owns that and understands

that it's not totally cool. So he's a bit more comfortable with me dating women.

This criticism of the conventional male undervaluation of female–female relationships as less threatening is reflected in the polyamorous dynamics. Mint (2008) notes how his polyamorous practice reflects a stereotypical straight man's fantasy to have two girlfriends, yet he is critical of such a patriarchal fantasy given his feminist leanings. He describes what Sheff (2006, 625) terms "poly-hegemonic masculinity," that is, "the idealized form of masculinity valorized" by having the attention of more than one woman. A variation of this dynamic was replicated among some of the queer women in my study in terms of butch and femme, as noted earlier by Alex, where a femme-femme dynamic was deemed less threatening.

Most polyamorists in my sample were critical of gender stereotypes in representations of jealousy yet at times also replicated them. Brianna stated that feminism used to influence her choices in polyamory, until the two were so integrated as to be indistinguishable. For her, identifying as polyamorous signalled a critique of dominant constructions of gender and sexuality.

> [Feminism] did [influence my choices] at the beginning, because I didn't want to engage in something that was somehow going to end up being biased against women or that was going to uphold patriarchal structures. But now I find that it doesn't, like my feminist beliefs don't play in in any way they wouldn't in the rest of my life, and in fact they play in less because it tends to be very egalitarian in my little world, very little gender stuff comes up, just once in a while someone gets reactionary and blames it on gender, but typically I don't experience that … Polyamorous people just think so much that they've already thought through gender, typically.

There is a significant overlap between polyamorous and bisexual communities and practices. Although many bisexuals eschew the stereotype that they must be non-monogamous in order to be "legitimately" bisexual, many do embrace polyamory (Ebin 2006; Klesse 2007). Rambukkana (2004, 141) found that in some social circles, there was a "pressure to be(come) bisexual within polyamory," which he compares to "a similar pressure within 1970s feminism to be(come) lesbian." Several of my participants who were bisexual or also dated men offered insight not into how the emotional experience of men differed from that of women but rather into how polyamorous culture differed from both queer culture and heterosexual culture, as well as how gendered interactions affected and influenced emotional states. For example, Alasia noted how hetero-sexual culture questioned gender and sexuality less than queer culture and how she was more compliant within her heterosexual relationship:

> I think I allowed a man more control of me out of his jealousy, at least when I was young. The father of my daughter, he was very jealous. He would be jealous of me going to see my mother. I don't think he was ever jealous of the baby, but he only lasted for 3 months. I only had the baby and realized he had to get out. I realized I gave him a lot of power. He was jealous of [my pursuits of] acting as well, which was what I wanted to be doing. And I accepted it.

Similarly, Heloise argued that jealousy had a lot to do with the way we are socialized to have relationships, instead of influencing solely the way a certain gender responded to a jealousy-provoking situation.

> My experience with the men that I have met has been that they are more jealous. They are more likely to have a negative reaction with their wife being with another person than the wife has with the man being with other people. It's funny because when you look at gay men, it doesn't seem to be there the same way … It may just be non-monogamy that's the issue. But from what I've read and stuff, it seems a little weird, because then it would indicate that it has nothing to do with male and female. It has something to do with heterosexual relationships.

Comparatively, Martha argued that men and women, monogamist or polyamorist, did not have different experiences of jealousy; rather,

> the context of it would be different. And I especially see that in differences between queer and heterosexual relationships … Men are expected to be a certain way in this culture. I'm tough and macho and I have it together. And it's such a patriarchal thing, but if that is threatened in any way, and it's threatened so easily, so the jealousy/fear is just boom, with aggression, with anger. I certainly think there is a difference in the way women and men express it, but the expression itself is similar, when you bring it to that primary [emotion] … of fear. Women are more inclined to nag and cry and men are more inclined to get angry and aggressive and partially that is socially constructed.

Martha connected the experience and expression of jealousy to the ways in which people related to each other, as circumscribed by gendered socialization into queer or heterosexual cultures. Coraline also described how jealousy was socialized vis-à-vis gender and perpetuated in Western culture:

> I think that a lot of jealousy is driven by our culture and driven by popular culture. I don't just think it, I know it. You wouldn't be able to see all those trash gossip magazines – that's what gossip is all about. It's about inspiring jealousy and reinforcing the feeling of inadequacy over all people so you can sell things to them. Simply … To me one of the driving keys of that cornerstone to it, is jealousy, to continue promoting the feeling of jealousy … and so I know heterosexually identified people experience jealousy differently because they are expected to … feel jealous, not just feel jealous in romantic relationships, but pretty much every relationship they have with every other human being … Having given my whole little dissertation there doesn't mean I'm immune to it. I certainly feel it. And it's really interesting being somebody who's always educated myself politically. I've always been politically involved and considered myself to be a social activist, but it doesn't make me immune to jealousy.

This quotation demonstrates the gap between theoretical critiques of dominant ideas and the actual emotions experienced, many of which are being worked through by polyamorists. Coraline implied that deconstructing jealousy was part of her social activism.

Tianna's experience of jealousy fit the conventional expectation that women's jealousy was triggered by emotional connection with other people, while men's jealousy was triggered by sexual connection. She experienced little jealousy when her partner had sexual connections with other people but found her partner's emotional connections with other people much harder. However, she personally did not want sexual relationships where the emotional connection was absent.

> I would be perfectly happy if [she] just picks up dates, fucked them for a little bit and never saw them again. But I tend to like deeper connections, so it's always easier on the other side of the fence … Part of it is that I tend to be more uncomfortable with deep intimacy [between my lover and her dates], so the sleepover thing … that's too intimate for me, the snuggling in bed and waking up and having coffee in the morning and watching each other brush your teeth and I think that again, it looks too much like my relationship and I wouldn't want that with anyone else.

Brianna described how many women, in her experience, fit the conventional description of jealousy but how this was challenged by polyamorists:

> I have had [female] friends say to me, "I don't know how you do it. I wouldn't mind if he slept with someone else, but I wouldn't want him to actually love them." Definitely I've seen that in other people who have come in and out of our lives, that we are fine with it as long as they thought that he didn't love, but when they realized that he loved me and the extent of that and the commitment then they were gone ... Some of the women that have come in and out have done that whole manipulation thing. But it's hard for me to say because people that are poly tend to discuss things openly and own these things rather than being manipulative because it would fail otherwise.

Polyamorists are actively critiquing the dominant gender rules regarding jealousy, even when they do match the conventional divide. Competition between women is exacerbated by dominant gendered models of jealousy, relationship models, and participation in subcultures. Another way in which polyamorists rethink jealousy is through relinquishing emotional control and attempting to ease competition.

Emotional Control

Holding on to anger is like grasping hot coal with the intent of throwing it at someone else; you are the one who gets burned.

Parkinson, Fischer, and Manstead (2005)

Get in touch with your fear. Get in touch with your heart.

Martha (study participant)

Classic Cartesian dualism pits reason against emotion and male against female. Reason is considered of utmost importance and emotion is seen as frivolous, something that needs to be controlled lest it get in the way of proper reason. Boler (1999, 109) argues

> that the deceptive opposition between a pedagogy that either *invites expression of feelings* or *engages in intellectual rigor* signals not a shortcoming within consciousness-raising practices. Rather, this indicates how deeply the oppositions between feeling and intellect are built into Western

paradigms and language that shape educational work and scholarship. (emphasis in original)

Polyamorists revere certain emotional experiences, particularly love, romance, and compersion, while they look down upon other emotionally driven experiences, such as jealousy, possessiveness, and competition. For polyamorists, there is a tension with regard to the emotion of jealousy: polyamorists claim jealousy to be a natural part of romantic life, yet jealousy is understood as a barrier to intimacy. So despite their belief that there should be no shame attached to experiencing jealousy, acting on jealousy in certain ways may be judged negatively. Although it may be considered a normal part of polyamorous experience, jealousy is also an emotion that, once worked through adequately, is thought to either dissipate or transform into a positive emotion. This is the emotional work often considered inherent in the polyamorous experience. Sometimes this emotional work is done by processing to reveal the deeper source of jealousy (what is it really about?) and communicating one's way through it. Supporting each other through jealousy often starts with a confession of jealousy in the hopes that this will dissipate or transform the emotion, or that one's partner will offer reassurance to mitigate the jealousy.

Emotions are sometimes seen as what takes over when one "loses control." Several of my participants discussed controlling the emotions that would otherwise lead to jealousy, and jealousy arising when this control had ceased. Emotional self-control is commonly portrayed as a masculine ideal and equated with self-mastery as well as mastery over others (Lupton 1998). Lupton notes that "a major binary opposition in discourse on emotion is that of the 'emotional woman' and the 'unemotional man'" (ibid., 105). In her research, Lupton found that people who thought themselves to be unemotional represented emotionality negatively. They often described emotion as a loss of control and their lack of emotion as an ability to "think before expressing one's feelings" (ibid., 46–7). By this logic, emotion is understood as what is expressed and what can be controlled rather than what is initially felt (which may be very strong). There was a general (although not mutually exclusive) divide among my participants – those who said they dealt with jealousy by allowing it to be experienced without imposing reason or control upon it and those who tried to control their jealousy in order to master and mitigate it. Janelle argued that polyamorous culture encouraged people to experience jealousy rather than deny it.

So just allowing yourself to even just be jealous is so much more freeing and you end up not being as jealous. And also being able to talk to your partner and say, "you know what? This threatens me or I need some reassurance, can you give that to me?" And it kind of just dissipates. Okay, I'm not so jealous anymore.

Other participants tried to understand jealousy rationally, by finding a reason for the emotion to occur. Francine described her ability to shift her emotional experience through rational control: "I'm someone who can totally tinker with my own thoughts." Orion also talked about managing jealousy through rationalization:

Rationality. I get the very rational side of my brain in gear. The rational side that says, this doesn't change that, this doesn't change that. I'm getting better at asking for what I need.

Similarly, Martha made a distinction between emotion and reason and used the split to dissipate her jealousy:

I have my embodied experience and I have my cognitive process … I say okay, this is a negative experience and it's either going to be hurt or fear and I start doing my logical deductions in my mind and it always comes down to fear for me. And I can do it like this [snap] because I have done it for so many years … that is what I do. Get in touch with your fear. Get in touch with your heart.

Some participants spoke of having the ability to choose whether or not they felt jealous. Priscilla explained that she could see a situation where jealousy might occur, and she would make a conscious choice as to whether or not she would feel it. For some people, jealousy was thought to be more legitimate when there was a direct reason. People look for reasons why they are jealous, such as their lover's actions or personal insecurities. When jealousy is perceived to be without reason, the person who feels it is then considered irrational, suspicious, or "crazy." When jealousy is based on a legitimate reason, it is seen as justified and thus reflects positively on the one who experiences it. Reasons, however, are often assigned after the emotion is experienced (Lehrer 2009). People are apt to infer reasons in a situation and to create a narrative where previously there was solely an affective experience, thus creating the dichotomy between emotion and reason after the fact or after the act.

Another element of the issue of control is how certain people attempt to control the actions of others when these actions have an emotional effect on themselves. Some polyamorists argue that the monogamous model is based on the control of other people's actions, often through possessiveness. Resistance to this aspect of mono-normativity was one core reason some of my participants chose to engage in polyamory. The following quote from Ren demonstrates how she saw the connection between gender, jealousy, ownership, and monogamy:

> I think in our society we're told to want what other people have. I think it's capitalism. I think it's misogyny. I think all of these things play into keeping us isolated and dependent on the systems. If I'm inadequate in whatever way, I just need to buy this thing ... And we're fed all this stuff and I think it's a lot about keeping people dependent on power structures and money and hierarchy ... It's constantly being reinforced, whether I look at a magazine or I see some heterosexist advertisement or whatever. There are still parts of me, even though I have been radicalized, politi-cized, trying to look at myself and question all of this and break down the status quo, it's still reinforced. There are still parts of me that think my body is not right. That love is not abundant and therefore I better hold on to it even if I don't like this situation, like I have to prove that I am better, like some competition that I'm better than this person. Like love is finite and whatever is finite. Like I need to hoard material goods and love because there is not enough. It's just tools of oppression and I think all of this monogamy and sexism and it all inter-plays in a way to keep us hating ourselves. And so we keep on buying things and staying in gross power dynamics.

In this comment, Ren demonstrated the connections between jealousy and fear of loss, fear of inadequacy, and fear of loneliness, as well as how some of these fears are perpetuated in Western culture. Ren also reflected the perspective some have of polyamory as a political practice.

Another aspect of emotional control is how jealousy can be triggered when someone does not feel as though they have control over a situa-tion. Tianna was aware of her tendency to try to control situations and how jealousy was spawned from this lack of control. "That's when I want to start to control things because I have a bit of a control issue." She argued that while she trusted her lover, she was unable to control what her lover's date was doing or her intentions. For Tianna, this was when her jealousy was most triggered:

> Part of what is hard for me is that, aside from the fact that when I'm doing something I know exactly what I'm doing and what it means to me, and I know exactly where I stand and what my intentions are. Hopefully I know what the other person I'm doing those things with is as well, because I know them and I trust them. And I'm in control of it. But when she's doing something, like you go walking on the beach and you say it's not a big deal and it's not intimate and it doesn't mean anything. But what if the girl walking with you does [think that]? And then she's getting mixed messages, and that's where my control stuff kicks in. But you're taking a femme down to the beach! Don't you understand that?

This example by Tianna speaks to trusting cohearts, the link between control and trust, and also the competition between femmes in the queer community. She had associated walks on the beach with a high level of romance and intimacy. Tianna said,

> I never trust the other person. I just don't. I don't trust people. And I don't trust femmes easily ... I think part of it that she is quite a catch. She's gorgeous, she's smart, she's funny, she's sweet, she's loving. She's got a good job, all these things ... There are 100 femmes behind me that would kill to have [her], right? ... It's not to say that I wouldn't have an unattractive, unintelligent partner, but ... there is a fucking scarcity of butches, goddamn it! And so I don't trust the other girl. Not just this one, but not any of them ever. I've never trusted them.

Later in the interview, Tianna disclosed that she did indeed trust the partner of her secondary lover, a femme woman who preceded her by several years with that lover. This kind of chronology was common in how people experienced jealousy. A person can come to trust relationships or obligations that existed prior to the relationship, as one may accept a partner's prior professional or familial obligations (Ben-Ze'ev and Goussinsky 2008). It was easier to trust the people who came before since the dynamic was already established and likely not to be changing. The people who come after are the ones that present unknown variables, with whom the trust and "control" is still tenuous.

The "scarcity of butches" that Tianna described referred to her sense that there were many more femmes than butches and that this skewed the dating pool (for those who dated within the butch/femme community), which contributed to her sense of competition among femmes. For Tianna, this "scarcity" was coupled with the privilege afforded to masculinity in the queer women's community. This situation makes for a small reversal of power relations in this limited sphere since, in dominant culture, feminine women are afforded more privilege than masculine and gender non-conforming women. Alyson was a butch and had this to say about the privilege of butches and sexual tops in this small slice of polyamorous culture, as well as about the responsibility that accompanied it:

> I actually think that because being a top in the world we live in is actually a position of privilege, that one actually gets to go around with a whole bunch of unexamined stuff that is either just fine or is somehow eroticized, so I don't think tops have to work on the painful parts as much as bottoms. Or as femmes do compared to butches or as anybody who is in social demand ... I think [about what] femmes settle for, like you can be an ignorant bastard butch and never be alone on a Saturday night. Where if you have the same behaviour and you were a femme, you could be exiled. And you can be a psychotic lunatic as a top and still never be alone on a Saturday night, and as a bottom, you are going to have a harder time. It's just the way the ratios break down and whatever internal, well sexism really, fuels both of those equations; top is better than bottom, butch is better than femme.

Alyson's sentiment also speaks to a parallel "scarcity" and privilege afforded to tops within the leather community (of which approximately two-thirds of my participants participated/identified), and thus competition between femmes and between bottoms, which can inspire jealousy. Tops are seemingly less common than bottoms (a very interesting fact in and of itself),[16] and this increases their position in the social hierarchy. This kind of power in the established pecking order of queer women, in terms of both gender and sexual power play, can translate into jealousy. Clanton (1996) describes the way these power relations play into experiences of jealousy. For example, the person who is assumed to be able to find a date more easily upon a break-up is afforded a degree of power

---

16   This finding is replicated in Klesse's (2007, 131) study where a bisexual male participant, in reference to the SM scene, described a "massive surplus of bottoms, people want to be dominated."

that can result in jealousy on the part of the other partner. Although Clanton's work comes from a monogamous model, it applies to poly-amory as well. If one member of a couple is highly sought after while the other is less so, this perception translates into power and can at times lead to a sense of vulnerability or jealousy. Thus, the people who are butch or tops in the leather, polyamorous community are more likely to be thought to have this kind of power. This power differential and its association with vulnerability is related to why Tianna was less trusting of femmes than of butches. Such power relations contribute to emotion-ally embodied affect and will be explored in the following chapter.

Conclusion

Re-imagining the connection between gender, jealousy, and monogamy can shift or mitigate the experience of jealousy. When the feeling rules of jealousy are softened, aspects of jealousy are reduced. Critiquing the convention and then recreating modes of interaction can shift the ways in which jealousy is embodied. Yet even after the social roots of jealousy are deconstructed and one attempts to cultivate compersion, the emotion can still persist. The potential for transformative emotional practices is significant. The barriers to the actualization of these poten-tials come not from human nature but rather from the structural and regulatory power constructions that are experienced emotionally. As described throughout this chapter, although my participants attempt to challenge mono-normative constructs of jealousy and gender, at times they replicate and reproduce these norms.

Through their polyamorous practice, my participants attempted to reclaim and revalue and revitalize sexual agency. This process was a cen-tral component by which my participants re-imagined the intersection of gender and jealousy. They critiqued jealousy's socially constructed connection to mono-normativity, heterosexism, genderism, and sex-ism, and through this critique they attempted to soften the power of the emotion. They tried to cultivate different emotional responses than those constructed in the emotion world of institutional monogamy, as a means of resistance. My research into polyamorous queer women offers insight into how a feminist approach to emotions can be actualized. In the following chapter, I continue the dialogue regarding the gendered rules of jealousy by focusing on the intersection of jealousy, power rela-tions, and sexuality as re-imagined, resisted, and practised by polyam-orous queer women.

5 Jealousy Can Be Hot if You Flip It: Working and Playing with Power

Everything in the world is about sex, except sex. Sex is about power.

Oscar Wilde

Power is the silly putty of my sexuality.

Courtney (study participant)

Jealousy is an emotion that emerges from social relationships, making it intricately tied to power relations. According to Klesse (2007, 115), "complex power relations structure *all* intimate and/or sexual relationships" (emphasis in original). Similarly, "emotionality as a claim *about* a subject or a collective is clearly dependent on relations of power, which endow 'others' with meaning and value" (Ahmed 2004b, 4; emphasis in original). Jealousy is linked to fear of loss of a relationship or of decline in its quality, and such changes in a relationship are embedded in power relations. My research into polyamorous queer women demonstrates that social ideas have embodied affect, and both social phenomena and their affect are malleable. In chapter 3, I described how polyamorists develop polyamorous culture with the intention of making the embodiment of compersion possible. In chapter 4, I explored how polyamorists re-imagine and recreate the gendered feeling rules of jealousy, again with the intention of shifting the experience of jealousy. In this chapter, I examine how polyamorists rethink their emotional lives in relation to power, both in their interpersonal relationships and in connection to institutional power structures. I am interested in how polyamorists respond to the emotion world of institutional monogamy by focusing on their emotional outcomes. In my sample population, I found that participants' cultivation of alternative models/uses of jealousy and compersion functioned as resistance to the sexual mores of the dominant culture, although at times they also reproduced the very structures they intended to avoid.

Certain contemporary literature posits same-sex relationships as transgressive vis-à-vis hegemonic power; in particular, same-sex relationships are seen as egalitarian in principle (Klesse 2007, 2). Similarly, current writing on polyamory often holds up polyamorous practice as a model of what Giddens (1992, 2) calls the pure relationship, that is, "a relationship of sexual and emotional equality" which emphasizes trustworthiness, self-reflexivity, and consensuality. Barker and Langdridge (2010b) argue that this perspective fits into a paradigm that positions polyamory as celebratory. This celebratory paradigm is potentially appealing: it makes queers seem more progressive and stands in contrast to the pervasive homophobia and heterosexism of past scholarship about sexual orientation. Similarly, this perspective positions polyamorists as inherently progressive and offers a positive outlook to oppose the invisibility of non-monogamy in discourse on relationships. However, as Klesse (2007, 2) points out, such a perspective leads to an "impoverished understanding of the complexity of power in intimate and sexual relationships and encounters." I agree that the celebratory paradigm does not account for this complexity, and it romanticizes polyamorous and same-sex relationships. It may be more useful to argue that "emotional equality" is an ideal rather than a descriptor of actual queer or polyamorous relationships. This goal is consistent with Weeks, Heaphy, and Donovan (2001, 109), who argue that, "the commitment to striving for an equal relationship ... is the prime characteristic of non-heterosexual ways of being."

Rather than rely on the idealistic equation of alternative sexualities/relationship patterns with emotional equality, I continue with my intersectional analysis and follow Klesse's (2007, 3) lead in challenging "single-issue analysis," instead looking at the "mutual interconnectedness of multiple forms of oppression." I re-conceptualize the concept of resistance in polyamorist practice. I try to avoid polarizing categories of good and bad, as well as assumptions that any one model of relationship is necessarily more progressive than another. I argue that the effect of power relations on polyamorists' experience of jealousy depends on how they live, interpret, and experience power as opposed to an abstracted notion of power imposed from the outside. Everyday experiences of power do not always correspond easily to theoretical constructions of power or to theories of jealousy. My view of the circulation of power in queer polyamory emerges from close analysis of participant transcripts and an attentive reading of their individual locations in the socio-sexual realm rather than from any a priori conception of power.

Power is ever-present in our lives yet is also intangible and challenging to identify. It emerges from an ever-shifting set of circumstances, relations, and interpretations of situations. To understand emotions, it is important to look at the "structure and process of power and status relationships between actors" (Kemper 2008, 128). While power relations can have definable features, as with financial matters and status, the extent to which *emotions* are affected by power also relies to a considerable degree on how power is perceived. Kemper (2008, 128) highlights this proposition when he writes, "*a very large class of human emotions results from real, anticipated, recollected, or imagined outcomes of power and status relations*" (emphasis in original). Thus, jealousy's embodiment result from a combination of one's position vis-à-vis intersecting power relations and institutional power structures, as well as the perception of one's own power in interpersonal relations.

In my research, I found that power's connection to the experience of jealousy is revealed through three overlapping manifestations, which are constantly at play in the production of emotions. First, power relations manifest in interpersonal dynamics, as they relate to class, gender, "race," ethnicity, age, beauty, quantity of partners, and other hierarchized structures. Second, institutional power is deployed through mono-normativity, heterosexism, and sexism. The third overlapping dimension is perceived power. One's perception of power is embodied in an individual's unique affective experiences and emotional responses to the interpersonal and social world. By extension, re-imagining how power is perceived (in the past, present, or future) can alter jealousy's affect (i.e., the physical sensations associated with jealousy and compersion). The perception of changing embodied power relations has embodied emotional outcomes. For example, if you perceive that your partner is unconditionally committed to you, you may be less likely to experience jealousy. This reaction is based on one's perception of the power dynamics in one's relationship(s), possibly independent of the partner's behaviour. The reverse can also occur: one's insecurity can be based solely on one's perception of a lack of power, again potentially independent of the partner's actions. At the same time, responding to this insecurity by expressing jealousy can shift power relations, shifts that are often marked by experiences of vulnerability, fear, and insecurity. The power plays evidenced in my sample offer insight into alternative ways of dealing with jealousy and thus alternative embodiments.

Notably, the use of the word "perceived" is not meant to dismiss the validity of jealousy's affect. Rather, I point to the importance of our interpretation of situations in the embodiment of its affect. Many people describe jealousy as a result of insecurity coming from an imbalance of power, real or perceived. Jealousy can be experienced as vulnerability linked to the fear of losing a relationship or of a decline in its quality, which again is inseparable from how one understands power within a relationship. For example, a person may not be threatened in their relationship, but their perception of an imbalance of power could trigger a jealous response. While power relations can have material affect, on an emotional level, perceptions of power play a formidable role in understanding one's position in a relationship and contribute to tangible emotional effects. Emotions emerge in ways independent of cognitive understandings of them. Contemporary neurological and psychological studies are finding not only that emotion and reason are intricately connected, but also that our perception of our circumstances can have a tangible impact on our brain's response, with corresponding embodied emotional results in an integrated biosocial feedback (Lehrer 2009; Siegel 2010).

In his relationship assessment model, Clanton (1996) suggests that how and when people experience jealousy is linked to the way power functions in interpersonal relationships. He connects power to circumstances such as who loves whom more, who is thought to be more likely to find another partner sooner upon break-up, who has access to more financial resources, etc. Some of these factors are tangible or materially based, whereas others rely on perception. In a polyamorous situation, if one's partner has a date with a new person, this is a tangible circumstance, but the potential for jealousy relies upon the ways in which one maps power relations upon this new relationship. Interpersonal power relations are intricately linked to one's sense of security in a relationship, which is connected to how and when one experiences jealousy. Jealousy is culturally associated with shame, low self-esteem, insecurity, and immature emotional development (Clanton 1996) – all things that can evoke a sense of vulnerability. Thus, exposing one's jealousy may exacerbate power differences, which in turn may increase one's jealousy.

In this chapter, I begin with a description of how polyamorists are affected by the regulation of sexuality and of emotions, and consequently how they respond to mono-normativity. I found that although some of their energy was directed towards advocating polyamory, the bulk of my sample participants were mainly concerned with how mono-normative standards affected them emotionally and sexually and how these standards can be restructured. For example, if one partner had a second partner and the other did not, instead of letting the hierarchy of this disparity interfere with their relationship, they tried to match the underlying desires rather than the surface actions that underlay this difference, so that "double standards" did not impede their relationship. Heloise explained,

> Being in a poly relationship and it being equal and balanced does not mean that each person has the same number of lovers and the same number of dates per month. It's about both of them having the relationship that they want even if it means one person not being poly at all and one person being poly ... It's about matching the standard to the person.

I also found examples of practical ways in which polyamorists worked with power imbalances as a means to minimize jealousy, and ways in which they played with pre-existing power imbalances that minimized the negative emotional affect of such power relations. Even as polyamorists try to construct their emotional and sexual lives around a polyamorous philosophy, dominant power structures replicated themselves in these relationships, in their interpersonal dynamics, in internalized polyphobia, and in the way consent was negotiated.

Institutional Power and Microaggressions: The Intersecting Regulation of Sexuality and Emotion

We are adventurers ... We want to know everything. Feel it all. See it all.

Dominique (study participant)

I see monogamy as dictated by an oppressive patriarchal culture.

Grace (study participant)

Pleasure, like power, is creative.

Ladelle McWhorter

Polyamorists attempt to re-craft their understanding of love, sexuality, relationships, and emotions in ways that minimize instances of jealousy and replace jealousy with compersion. This reframing challenges the idea that sexual exclusivity is the epitome of love and commitment and that any digression from this path should be met with distrust and jealousy. Instead, polyamorists reframe jealousy as an emotion that is neither inevitable nor intolerable, and they negotiate the parameters of their relationships accordingly. Polyamorists re-imagine their relationships and create new norms and strategies that steer their practice as a culture, as opposed to solely individually. These rules include ways to initiate communication, negotiate boundaries, structure disclosure (as described in chapter 3), question gender norms (as was the focus in chapter 4), and most importantly for this chapter, rethink power relations. While not always ensuring successful compersion in practice, these ideas inform the culture of polyamory and the position of polyamorists in a mono-normative world. In this section, I discuss how polyamorists are affected by the regulation of emotion and sexuality and how these two modes of regulation intersect. Social regulation operates across the domains of sexuality and emotion; the experience of emotion affects and is affected by sexual practice. Such regulation was reflected by Courtney:

> In order to go through the process of having come out as queer, come out as kinky, some out as poly, we'd had to deliberately make the step to become visibly something that isn't normal, which is always dangerous in a social sense.

Mono-normative culture operates through the intersecting formal and informal regulation of emotions and sexuality. With regard to compulsory monogamy, Haritaworn, Lin, and Klesse (2006, 518) argue that

> individuals and communities engaging in polyamorous practices are forced to negotiate monogamist normativities which pathologize them as untrustworthy partners and dysfunctional parents. These judgments are based in wider contexts of sex negativity which demonize all but a few practices and desires involving a small range of gendered bodies.

For example, polyamorists are barred from legally marrying their multiple spouses and some polyamorists have faced custody battles over their children (see Sheff 2013). Some forms of informal regulation are microaggressions, gossip, teasing, and invisibility, all of which contribute to polyamorists remaining closeted, which in turn bolsters mono-normativity. Another example of the informal regulation of emotion is the frequent presentation of love as synonymous with monogamy. For example, the lyrics in many love songs equate true love with the exclusion of other people or qualify love in comparison with other people (Ben-Ze'ev and Goussinsky 2008). Although many polyamorists are able to persist without direct social regulation (i.e., most polyamorists are not directly punished for their behaviour),

> consensual non-monogamies continue to be demonized, pathologized, marginalized and subject to the social regulation of ridicule ..., with no legal protections for people involved (for example, around child-care or relationship status). (Barker and Langdridge 2010b, 756)

Furthermore, Weeks (1985, 27) argues,

> Five broad areas stand out as being particularly crucial in the social organization of sexuality: kinship and family systems, economic and social organization, social regulation, political interventions, and the development of cultures of resistance.

Polyamorists are affected by all these areas with regard to both regulation and resistance. Polyamorists resist the nuclear family system by constructing family units with multiple partners, often with alternative economic organization. For example, some polyamorists have legally incorporated their families to circumvent the monogamous financial familial arrangement, enabling them to operate under corporate rather than familial legalities. Polyamorists resist dominant regulatory bodies that structure monogamous marriage as natural and normal. Building on Weeks's list, I add the regulation of emotions. The regulation of sexuality contributes to the ways in which emotions are socialized and in turn embodied. Love is deeply embodied yet emerges within particular cultural parameters. "Emotions make culture meaningful and give it the power to regulate conduct" (Turner and Stets 2005, 292). The feeling rules of jealousy are intertwined with those of sexuality. I found that polyamorists created a culture of resistance to the dominant sexual model by developing their own set of subcultural practices, with the goal of shifting emotional outcomes. In other words, they resisted sexual regulation by shifting their emotional practices.

Although polyamory is mostly invisible within mono-normative culture, the subject has recently received mainstream media, including the notable television show on Showtime, *Polyamory: Married and*

Dating. Much of the media coverage has portrayed polyamory from an angle which downplays the sexual and focuses instead on the romantic and emotional aspects. Polyamorists have equally participated in this slanted portrayal (see Mint 2007b). Even if it is delivered for its shock value, for its "edgy," or potentially comedic, spin, this mainstream attention is significant in that it acknowledges an alternative to the normative values of the nuclear family. It should also be noted that this mainstream attention exists as part of the widespread increasing commercialization of sexuality and thus should not necessarily be read as acceptance.

Although Vancouver has seen some polyamorous activism,[17] most of the discourse has been inwardly focused, with an emphasis on the development of information to support polyamorous practice and to counter adverse emotional and sexual effects of mono-normativity, as well as social networking. The bulk of polyamorous literature to date emphasizes "how to" instructions on polyamory as well as clinical counselling care. My sample exemplified this tendency in that participants, in part, resisted mono-normative culture by focusing on emotional practices rather than through opposition to formal regulation. The Internet has been a central medium for generating and sharing information on polyamory, allowing polyamorists to circumvent other barriers to organizing that have been problematic for past sexual movements, such as censorship or reliance on dominant media to publicize information. Connecting via the Internet has sped up the circulation of information, enabling polyamorists to connect with one another without being limited by geography, eventually reaching a critical mass of discourse and networking. An increase in visibility, however, does not necessarily translate into social acceptance. Public knowledge of polyamory is indeed a double-edged sword. Increased awareness may decrease misconceptions and contempt, or conversely, it may draw attention to a practice that some people consider sexually deviant.

Being out about one's polyamorous practice, particularly at work and in some family situations, can make polyamorists vulnerable to derision or even discrimination. My participants talked about how challenging it can be to remain closeted about a significant part of one's life while everyone else is able to talk with ease about their one and only partner. It takes conscious effort to exclude names from a narrative or to have

---

17   Such as the Canadian Polyamory Advocacy Association (http://polyadvocacy.ca/) and the Vancouver Canadian Polyamory social group (www.vanpoly.ca).

to choose which partner to bring to a function, forcing polyamorists to lie, omit, or come out. Several of my participants noted that being in the marginal position made them realize the frequency with which mention of one's significant other came up in casual conversation.

Polyamorists are affected by assumptions, misconceptions, and sometimes public scorn, which emerges from the emotion world of mono-normativity as well as sex-negativity. Polyamorists are subject to microaggressions, which are intentional or unintentional subtle expressions of indignity that convey disapproval or hostility (see Sue et al. 2007). While microaggressions tend not to be physically aggressive, their challenge is that on the surface they appear innocuous. When discrimination is covert, it can sometimes be challenging to confront since it requires more explanation. For example, a micro-invalidation occurs when a polyamorists must choose only one of their significant others to bring to a work function or declare on their relationship status on a social networking website. Another example is when a polyamorist will identify a lover as a friend, thus trivializing or misleading others about the real nature of their relationship. Such subtle alienations function cumulatively to further marginalize poly-amorists, often pushing polyamorists to hide their practice. Micro-aggressions also function on an emotional level, often perpetuating shame, stigma, and fear.

One way to interpret informal regulation comes from the reactions my participants received from people to whom they disclosed their polyamorous practice. For example, Courtney relayed a case of people succumbing to mono-normative assumptions of what qualifies as valid love, which had the effect of minimizing her relationships:

> I've had people ask me how I can tell my lovers apart. I've had people tell me that poly is okay but they couldn't be poly because they really loved their lovers.

Similarly, Janelle discussed the stigma attached to polyamory:

> It's probably harder to explain than being queer. And people mock ... I think there is some stigma attached to poly as well. It's the same response you get when you tell people you are bi. There is no legitimacy. It's like, you can't commit so you are poly. Or it must be your partner who is putting pressure on you. Or you must not love that person.

When she has talked about poly to non-poly people, Leigh has been told,

> Oh, so you're cheating? You are having an affair and you have to get out of the relationship. You must not love this person … That it's based on lies … That's for people who don't want to make a commitment.

Heloise noted more misconceptions:

> That you can't make up your mind. That you are taking the easy way out … Misconception that there is a good guy and a bad guy in the relationship, and this is usually the association of the person who is more actively poly … [People tell me that] it's the folly of the young … Do it while you are still young because when you get to my age you are just not going to have the energy for that.

Stigma can lead to minority stress, which refers to the pressure one undergoes as a result of social marginalization of their practice, through either direct prejudice, fear of prejudice, lack of social support, or internalization of stereotypes. Minority stress is also a significant adverse social determinant of health. One strategy for resisting informal regulation was exemplified by Courtney, who chose an unapologetic stance in order to avoid the shame and stigma of being accidentally outed.

> Start out and stay out. I don't need to shock anybody. There is nobody who doesn't know. Everybody is my friend because they know who I am. And dark sides as well. And that is really important to me because I don't fear exposure. I don't hide anything. I don't need to look for whether I left the paddle on the dining room table, when my friends come over, I just let them in. And my kink and poly are just a part of me like how I keep a messy house. Like the fact that I dote on my cats so much, like the fact that I don't dust more than once every six months, like the fact that I read a lot of books and have a boot fetish. All this stuff is part and parcel of who I am. And so being poly and being queer and being kinky is just a part of that. No point in hiding it.

It is important to note that Courtney was in a privileged position as a white, urban, able-bodied, educated queer woman. The ability to live openly as polyamorous is affected by race, class, ability, and geography. It is much easier to live polyamorously in an urban area than in a rural environment, because of the size of one's dating pool, the social anonymity afforded to cities, and the ways in which (some) cities tend to support alternative sexualities. Although their socio-economic backgrounds varied significantly, my sample comprised people who had enough privilege or education (or perhaps chutzpah) to be able to persevere with polyamory, which then also influenced their approach to processing jealousy, a kind of emotional privilege. Polyamorists require cultural and social capital, as well as autonomy to support their lifestyle in the face of marginalization. Polyamorists require enough (leisure) time to develop their relationships as well as to permit them access to knowledge and resources.

Indeed, Ravenscroft (2004, 2) notes the following:

> If a given person identifies with the term "polyamorous," chances are that she or he is a citizen of the United States, raised in a middle-class household by a nominally Christian family with moderate-to-poor communication skills, where folks were loving and supportive but not great at showing how they felt ... He or she is most likely of high intelligence, has spent two or three years in college, is conversant in technology and the Internet.[18]

Although many polyamorists do not quite fit this categorization (myself included), the culture of polyamorous discourse tends to exemplify these values. As well, the language associated with a great deal of polyamorous literature is more accessible to white, Anglophone, middle-class, and Western readers. Polyamorists, as Rambukkana (2010, 238) makes clear, are never "just polys" and as such are both participants and recipients of multiple sites of privilege and penalty. For example, while polyamorists may be the recipients of microaggressions in a mono-normative culture, they at times also perpetuate microaggressions against secondary lovers and use power relations for their own benefit. (For more on diversity, privilege, and penalty of polyamorists, see Barker and Langdridge 2010a; Noël 2006; Rambukkana 2010; Sheff 2013.)

Polyamory developed partly in response to a critique of institutionalized monogamy and it exists on the margins of social acceptability, but polyamorists nevertheless at times reproduce white, middle-class, and Western emotional discourse. Nora, for instance, was stuck in a

---

18 Notably, his work is definitely American-centric. Since the publication of Ravenscroft's work, there has been increasingly more polyamory discourse outside of the United States.

challenging polyagony moment and her struggles were exacerbated by another layer of difference, this time difference from the polyamorous norm. In the following scenario, she describes the sexual confidence required to fit into polyamory's standard expression of self-assuredness and how this differed from her upbringing. Nora noted,

> That's something that is strongly culturally perpetuated for me in my own history. I'm Asian and that guilt and inadequacy is something that is hard-wired into me and always has been. And so I acknowledge that and my culture has many great aspects to it, but that particular set of component isn't particularly useful in this cultural context. Nor is it useful in a poly context at all. So I have those feelings and they feel pretty terrible.

The contemporary standard of polyamory requires a particular kind of direct communication regarding one's sexual and emotional needs, whereas Nora's background socialized her with a more indirect way to communicate and demonstrate love. Her "grungies" (i.e., poly-agony) were exacerbated by the clash between the feeling rules of her upbringing and the feeling rules of polyamory. To the extent that polyamorous culture is dominated by middle-class white people, the feeling rules that have developed may be more comfortable for certain polyamorists.

To several participants in my study, practising compersion itself was considered an act of resistance to sex-negative culture because it priori-tized pleasure and the body, which stands in contrast to the dictates of mono-normative values. Bronski (1998) notes that mainstream culture holds a paradoxical view of pleasure. On the one hand, pleasure is mar-keted as a consumeristic pursuit. On the other hand, Western culture upholds a long tradition of sex-negativity, which manifests in rules of acceptable sexual and social behaviour. We may be bombarded with por-trayals of sexuality but mostly in forms that are contrived and artificial, while representation of authentic sexual pleasure are scarce. For example, a movie might portray people dressed provocatively and connote sex within a one-minute scene, but engaged intimate foreplay that focuses on women's pleasure is unusual. Pleasure is restricted to being an incentive or reward, which must be rationed and partaken of only in small doses. Hence by prioritizing sexual and emotional pleasure, polyamorous prac-tice is a powerful reaction to the mono-normative emotional world.

Halperin (1995, 60) writes, "To resist is not simply a negation but a creative process." Queer politics, he argues, are not only reactionary but also creative in their production of alternative ways to live, thus politicizing self-transformative practices of sexuality and bodily pleasures. Foucault wrote that "self-invention is not a luxury or pastime … it is a necessity" (quoted in Halperin 1995, 81). For example, Foucault positions sadomasochism (SM) as subversive in its transformation of pain into pleasure and its decentralization of sexual intercourse. Foucault argued that SM practitioners were praiseworthy because they "invent new possibilities of pleasure with strange parts of the body" (quoted in Bersani 1995, 79). Thus, sadomasochism is a creative form of sexuality and a process of invention that transforms pre-existing power into pleasure (ibid.).

Approximately two-thirds of the participants in my sample stated that they engaged in some form of kink or BDSM. Many who did not engage in SM noted that their polyamorous practice was informed by SM discourse, such as the discourse of "safe, sane and consensual" play (see Sheff and Hammers 2011). My participants played with power in ways that paralleled SM practices in that they took power that already existed in the larger world and in their relationships and worked with it instead of against it. The overlap between polyamory and kink is significant in that both are subject to similar regulations of the body, both convert dominant ideas of power into acts of pleasure, and both maintain a playful approach to mitigating challenging emotions.

One of my participants, Coraline, saw the overlap between polyamory and SM this way:

> Identifying as a leatherdyke specifically is about identifying yourself as being sexual. I haven't met a leatherdyke yet who just wore leather for the sake of wearing leather. It's a signal saying "I'm sexual."

This quote from Coraline highlights the keen interest in sexuality shared by polyamorists and their strong affiliation with sex-positive discourse. Leigh argued,

> I believe we do D/S [dominant/submissive play] because there is power imbalance everywhere and we just actually acknowledge it and work with it consensually. Because everywhere we live there's power imbalance in everything we do. And the only difference between that outside and what we do is consent. And we actually acknowledge it and we do it in a cognitive sense. How does that relate to poly? Well, when we are doing well, I think it relates in the way Dominique just wants me to be happy.

By happiness, Leigh was referring to her and her partner's pursuit of other lovers to fulfil their kink-related desires. Leigh and Dominique transformed existing power structures into acts of pleasure in their polyamorous relationships.

On the overlap between sadomasochism and polyamory as it merges in acts of pleasure, Dominique pronounced,

> I think we like to explore and we like to travel. I think those are places you can do that in. We are adventurers ... I think we just really want to explore. We want to know everything. Feel it all. See it all.

Similarly, Cheyenne said,

> There's a big overlap between the ways we want to fuck and who we want to fuck and with how many people and what the dynamics are. It's about feeling it out and finding your own path. And just being really true to yourself and not feeling locked in if that's important. If who you are is about all these other paths, then really exploring them ... And so I end up gravitating towards the people who are even pushing those boundaries. Just saying whoa, there is not just one way of living outside the box and we all need to support one another because we can't start creating these exclusive communities because that's what we are trying to fight against. I don't feel like there is always an easy path in those communities. You always have to find the people who are pushing it sometimes a step further.

Cheyenne demonstrated how she built community with both polyamorists and other people who explore alternative sexualities. Klarissa described the overlap between poly and kink this way:

> One is that you have broken down the barriers in your mind about what is real sex and what is pleasurable. If you are able to get beyond the missionary position in your mind and say I'm into power ... If you are secure enough in yourself and are open to those things then it naturally leads to ... I mean they told me that missionary position married sex was the only thing, well I got beyond the missionary position, then maybe married is not the only thing, which naturally leads to breaking down barriers. The second thing is that especially with kinky stuff is that it's extremely unlikely that one person is going to give you everything you think and want. You might fall completely in love with someone who is

squicked[19] by needles and you might love to be pierced. And so it's very easy for someone to say you know what, I can't give you this but I know someone who can who I trust so I will "let you" get that from someone else ... I think that leads to ideas about how maybe I don't have to be sexually exclusive.

Klarrisa pointed to a common defence of polyamory – namely, that one person is unlikely to meet all one's emotional or sexual needs, and that by being polyamorous, one can have their needs met through other relationships. Klarrisa extended this argument beyond simple needs to include pleasure and sex. Martha also referred to a slippery slope argument:

> It really coincides with my queerness because for so long I repressed this massive part of myself and then coming out of that box, I'm like fuck this! I'm going to fuck whoever I want. Man, woman, tranny, I don't care!

This idea parallels Rubin's (1993) description of the cultural assumption of the "domino theory of sexual peril," which is the sexual axiom that once one cultural norm has been transcended, people are often comfortable pushing down other walls. Notably, Rubin disputes the assumption that one must transcend another boundary once one has pushed past a particular line and suggests instead that we interrogate the constructions of sexual morality that configures the good/bad dichotomy by developing the concept of "benign sexual variation" (Rubin 1993, 15).

In contrast to earlier Klarrisa's argument that polyamorists pursue second lovers to fulfil a need lacking with another lover, Courtney rebuked,

> Speaking of poly myths, the piece of the pie poly myth that my needs and wants are a pie and my lover is only perhaps able to pass half of my pie and so therefore my other pie must be eaten by people who have different things to offer me than my partner. Now this sounds really nice and people say it all the time and it is such utter horse-shit ... I don't have a lover and think, oh, I wish I could get my need for honesty met from my lover. I better find someone who can go be honest with me. I don't say well I have great sex with my lover, but I don't love them so I better get my love needs met ... I don't have any of these thoughts. What I do instead if

---

19   By "squicked," she meant physically disturbed.

I have someone in my life that I am attracted to and I pursue that attraction by getting to know them better. If I get to know them better and I am still attracted to them and they are attracted to me then we might have sex ... It's not because I see them as fulfilling some interesting need that I may or may not have in my hypothetical pie.

People engage in multiple relationships not solely to fill a lack in another relationship, but also because they are attracted to more than one person.

In the process of rejecting dominant models of sexual practice as a form of social resistance, some polyamorists undertook a protective stance by privileging poly over monogamy, often in connection to the idea that poly requires progressive emotionality. Coraline noted that the rejection of monogamy can itself be judgmental and reproduce hierarchies:

So the thing I was saying earlier about how in the poly community and judging people who are monogamous – that's a form of jealousy. Really at the root of it, it's about the fear of other and fear of other is usually based on some power dynamic and so I realize that at a certain underlying level, jealousy is fear and fed by fear that it's really easy for me to judge the wealthy, to judge the Right ... But what it really is, is jealousy about a power dynamic, which is ultimately about fear about an unequal power dynamic.

Coraline also discussed how true polyamory was difficult and that there was hypocrisy in the polyamorous world:

We are still very constrained by the whole model, the whole binary of monogamy and it makes it difficult for people to actually talk about poly. It's really easy for us to sit here and have this – an abstracted very logical conversation about poly. But let us actually sit at this table and talk about say ourselves or friends that we know who are actually having a difficult time with poly and I find unfortunately that even people who are really poly-positive, practising poly themselves, start to trot out really judgmental stuff that actually belongs to the old binary.

Coraline's quotation demonstrates one way in which mono-normativity influences polyamorous dynamics, even as polyamorists try to resist it. Coraline implied that a lack of jealousy in polyamorous practice was equated with being politically progressive. And yet, regardless of their rejection of dominant models of sexual practice and emotional normativity, polyamorists were not immune to jealous feelings. The "binary" here refers to the construction of good versus bad sexuality. Thus, by claiming that polyamory is a more evolved, freeing, and exciting way to conduct a relationship, one would perpetuate the very hierarchical and coercive dynamics polyamorists vocally reject. Another example is how some polyamorists distance themselves from and look down on swingers, even though the practices have a great deal in common.

Given that open relationships have become the accepted norm in certain subcultures, such as the leather community, a certain privilege is afforded to polyamorists. Alyson argued that a monogamist would have trouble finding a date in the leatherdyke community. Coraline stated that the "posturing of poly cool" functioned as a transvaluation of values, privileging polyamorists over monogamists. Thus, power is never a static possession. Instead, power and status shift in relation to particular permutations and affiliations that have bodily and discursive effects.

Institutional mono-normativity also affects polyamorists through the internalization of polyphobia. Polyamorous people sometimes complain about how it is challenging to come out to people, particularly families and co-workers. There are real consequences that come from being labelled a sexual deviant, including exclusion from family, loss of employment, and having children apprehended. Often polyamorists fear being stereotyped as promiscuous, immature, or unable to settle down. Hence, sometimes judgments polyamorists make against one another come from an internalization of this polyphobia or from the shame attached to transgressing mono-normativity. Ren noted the following internalization of polyphobia:

> My date had dated other people, but it's a lot different if it's a family unit living together because all of a sudden that's the big heavy, that's when people take it seriously because it's money and rent and bills and babies are involved. Like woah, that's a real relationship. Like that's somehow the valid one.

Ren was describing how non-poly people often think polyamory is an immature stage that will shift once one enters into a relationship with "real" responsibilities. Although she was critical of this logic, it still affected her thought process and caused her a sense of shame. So while polyamorists do actively critique mono-normativity, at times they also internalize and replicate the values of the dominant culture in their emotional responses. The ways polyamorists respond to institutional power also intersects with how they work and play with power in their interpersonal relationships.

Interpersonal Power within Relationships

Jealousy – that jumble of secret worship and ostensible aversion.

Emile M. Cioran

Although power is mobile and does not attach to a particular person, power does have physical and emotional effects. Clanton (1996) argues that jealousy results from an imbalance of power and suggests that the minimization of jealousy can be achieved from a move towards equalization of power in relationships. This section responds to the following questions: In the context of polyamorous relationships, how does perceived power and its re-imagining translate into jealousy or compersion? How does working through power shift the experience of jealousy? What kinds of power emerge in polyamorous relationships and how do polyamorists work with/through such power? Can playing with power shift one's experience of jealousy? Can jealousy be overcome in ways other than balancing out power?

Nobody Wants to Get Demoted: Perceptions of Power

Whether or not one person in a relationship has a discernible manifestation of power, the perception of a power imbalance in some circumstances can lead to actual emotional affect. For example, the person with more dates or more significant dates may be thought to hold a certain kind of power. The person who experiences more jealousy may be thought to have less power, and this is due in part to how being jealous exposes, or potentially exacerbates, one's vulnerability in a dynamic. Power is also particularly precarious at the start and at the end of a relationship, when roles and commitments are less known, less secure, or in flux. For some people there is more jealousy at the start of a relationship because the dynamics are uncertain and one is likely to be unfamiliar with the person. For others, there is less jealousy at the start because there is not as much investment in the relationship and potentially more limerence chemistry to override feelings of doubt or fear.

Most situations which correspond to heightened jealousy and insecurity are connected to perceived power relations. When a partner in an existing relationship starts dating someone new, there is often a shift in dynamic between the couple(s) and a degree of uncertainty regarding the outcome. Regarding age, an older person has a certain potential or perceived power connected to experience and wisdom, while youth holds a powerful physical appeal, especially in a culture obsessed with youthful beauty. In queer women's dynamics, there are also power differentials associated with masculinity and femininity. Feminine women are more culturally acceptable, but masculine women, in some limited queer circles, hold another kind of cultural privilege (Halberstam 1998).

Power is also tied to sexuality; the person who wants sex less may be thought to have more power (Clanton 1996). The person who is thought to be more sought after sexually by people outside the relationship may be perceived to hold more power. Furthermore, social, sexual, and physical power can be very attractive qualities. Power relations are possibly also be tied to the way attachment styles play out. For example, a person with a secure attachment style could hold more power than one with an anxious attachment style (see Levy and Kelly 2010). Martha argued, "There is a particular attachment style called the dismissive avoidant attachment style and the people who don't experience jealousy might fit the bill of that particular attachment style." It is also possible that a person with an avoidant attachment style will be thought to hold more power than a person with either secure or anxious styles. Between cohearts, there is power connected with closeness/affectional ranking (primary versus secondary). There may also be a status/hierarchy associated with which relationship began first. A person who has been one's lover longer holds a certain kind of seniority and a depth of connection, but a new lover has the appeal of new relationship energy and possibly an appeal unhindered by complications and logistics that can proceed from long-term relationships. Grace noted,

> Sometimes I get jealous of my new dates' new dates ... I just don't like the new exciting stage to be over, ever with anyone and I feel as soon as there is introduction of someone new, that symbolizes an overness.

Power relations play out in negotiations of time, such as who gets to attend certain functions with whom or who has dates for certain holidays or vacations. Socio-economic, financial, and career status are also connected to power relations, typically revealing themselves in conventional hierarchies. Similarly, a person's physical and mental health may contribute to power relations, as might a person's physical beauty, popularity, and social connections. A person who has more experience with polyamory may be thought to be more powerful. All such power relations do not add up to a simplistic equation but rather intersect in a multiplicity of ways with a variety of outcomes. Power is neither a possession nor a zero-sum game, yet how power manifests and is understood can translate into feelings of jealousy or compersion.

Courtney argued that "people sometimes define power as who is most or least willing to break off the relationship." Martha stated that power was inversely related to who liked whom more. She claimed the one who loved less or had less investment in the relationship had more power:

> I want this person to really be into me. Like really be into me. And I don't want them to know how much I am into them, because that feels too vulnerable. There's this fear that, oh I don't want to put in too much too soon. What if I am overbearing? What if it's too much? What if it's smothering? And I really want you to be into me.

Such imbalances and uncertainties about a partner's degree of affection can lead to experiences of jealousy. Similarly, Heloise described being jealous concerning her secondary lover: "She is more powerful, I am more in love with her than she is in love with me." Regarding other inequalities, Alasia said,

> That long-time lover of mine was also the more powerful one in the relationship. She wanted sex less often. She had more money. She had more time. So it might be just connected to power that you get to express your anger. So it might not be just with men, but men are more likely to have more power, socio-economically.

The dynamics that Alasia described are applicable to monogamous relationships as well, but the practice of polyamory further complicates power dynamics by adding more people into the mix. Celia described a situation in which material ownership translated into a power dynamic. She lived with her partner and his lover, the two of whom owned a house together. This was not necessarily a source of jealousy, but it contributed to power relations:

> I'm thinking more in terms of feeling threatened or insecure or worried about being replaced or worried about not being necessary. And those kinds of doubting your place.

Ren described power in relationships as being related to levels of affection, role, and time. She noted that "when one person is more emotionally invested than the other, that's a power dynamic and it can definitely bring out jealousy." Ren also observed that, in BDSM dynamics, power was discussed more explicitly than in polyamorous negotiation.

> With power roles within kink stuff, it's easier to lay it on the table than "how much do you like me? What percentage do I occupy in your heart or your time? Oh, you see that person twice a week, but you only see me once a week." Whatever … People don't want to be demoted and how much time [is spent together represents value].

Ren indicates that an explicit discussion of power could reduce the negative consequences of such power, but she also listed more factors connected to power and jealousy, including time spent together, factors that may not lessen jealousy even if they were deliberated outright. Indeed, many issues cannot be worked through. Ren linked power and thus potential jealousy to differing skills, emotional investment, and time. She brought up a significant point about how important are recognizable potential outcomes of power – loss, fear of loss, or demotion.

Labriola (2013) argues that there are "three circles of poly hell": demotion, displacement, and intrusion. Demotion refers to a de-ranking in the hierarchy of relationships, whether a drop from primary to secondary, an emotional detachment, or potentially a break-up. Displacement implies logistics, such as having less time and space with a partner. Intrusion refers to a partner's attention being diverted elsewhere, such as a lover being distracted by another person, either by limerence or potentially as a result of drama within the relationship. Several participants noted feeling jealous in regard to the way their partner would talk about a new lover, or as one participant called it, "all goggly eyed." For example, Heloise stated,

> The other hardest thing is that when you first fall in love or in lust or whatever it is, when we are first attached with a new person, you really do think about them all the time. And to be responsible to your partner, you can only sort of mention them once for every 10 times you think about them, which is still about 50 times a day … You constantly talk about them.

Because of the upfront negotiations required for polyamory to function smoothly, polyamorists acknowledge the importance of directly confronting issues associated with power in a polyamorous dynamic. Nora discussed how imbalances of power impeded her ability to be poly:

We don't split things to the centre or anything like that, but that equality is fundamental to our trust really. If there isn't that equality and that power, if one person has more power than the other I find that I'm in danger of feeling disempowered. And when I feel disempowered, that has a really bad effect on the rest of my life. Disempowerment for me feels like a loss of agency. And once I've lost agency, how am I supposed to negotiate poly with any sort of authority whatsoever?

Nora described agency as being contingent upon equal division of emotional and negotiating power but not upon equalizing features associated with power. In the previous example, Nora did not try to confront power by forcing herself and her partner to have the same experience; rather she looked for a way to address the emotional outcomes that are an effect of the perceived power imbalance. Courtney noted one outcome of sensing a lack of power: "Catty and manipulative is passive aggressive and passive aggressive behaviour comes out when you don't think you have any real power." Indeed, power relations translate into behaviour and modes of communication. Although polyamorous discourse emphasizes the importance of processing one's emotions, the act of negotiating jealousy in certain situations can also place an individual in an emotionally vulnerable position.

Jealousy and Vulnerability

Feelings like disappointment, embarrassment, irritation, resentment, anger, jealousy, and fear, instead of being bad news, are actually very clear moments that teach us where it is that we're holding back. They teach us to perk up and lean in when we feel we'd rather collapse and back away. They're like messengers that show us, with terrifying clarity, exactly where we're stuck. This very moment is the perfect teacher, and, lucky for us, it's with us wherever we are.

Pema Chodron

According to Lauren Berlant (2006, 20), "When we talk about an object of desire, we are really talking about a cluster of promises we want someone or something to make to us and make possible for us." Berlant argues that when we enter relationships or when we say, "I love you," we are implying a promise of loving and being together in the future as well. With the expectation of a future in a relationship comes the potential for loss. The power implicit in a potential loss can make one feel very vulnerable. To expose oneself as feeling jealous may seem like a declaration of the other person's power, potentially exacerbating the (sensation of) vulnerability. One partner's expression of jealousy can be interpreted as the other person having power, or it can shift perceived power. In mainstream culture, jealousy on the part of a partner can be interpreted as a sign of care or love, but for polyamorous people, a partner's jealousy is more often seen as a barrier to intimacy, in that it gets in the way of closeness and makes polyamorous practice more challenging. Thus, demonstrating or exposing vulnerability can exacerbate the intensity of jealousy.

As Alasia cleverly noted, "it takes two people to start a relationship, but it only takes one to end it." In other words, the "power of goodbye" is indeed the ultimate resolve. Experiencing jealousy may be cause to leave the relationship, and at other times a partner's jealousy may lead to the demise of the relationship. Courtney noted how many of her relationships "ended because of jealousy, but this jealousy was not mine." Alyson stated that experiencing jealousy in regard to her long-term lover's new date made her feel like the "old shoe" while the new coheart was "shiny and easier," as the new relationship did not yet require much emotional work. Jealousy, however, is not solely experienced in the realm of suspicion. In several instances, the jealous partner's suspicions were true, and the other person did leave her/him for the other lover, thus presenting a case of fait accompli jealousy.

The vulnerability experienced in conjunction with jealousy is connected to jealousy's assumed root in low self-esteem. Jealousy is tied to self-esteem when people connect infidelity to "injured honor" (Baumgart 1990, 121). This sense of injured honour may explain why one's jealousy is so often targeted at the "rival" rather than one's lover. In polyamory, this sense of injured honour may not be related to an adulterous partner since outside relationships are known and consensual. However, the sexual acts or promiscuity of one's partner may still be linked to shame. Orion experienced jealousy as embarrassment she would feel when other people saw her partner behaving in a sexually overt manner with someone else:

> I would just be sick with jealousy. But a lot of it was about embarrassment, like I remember being at a party with her and Toby and she had all these marks all over her from getting down with him, and I was so scared of people watching my reaction to what was so obviously really overt sexuality with somebody else. So I was very guarded and … I was really concerned with saving face over people who were watching me have to be face-to-face with their relationship.

Orion's sentiments also point to a sense of shame about being polyamorous, which connects to internalized polyphobia and mono-normativity. She may have been projecting monogamous values onto her polyamory, and hence experiencing shame that her partner appears not to be under her control or that she was being disrespected, and this shame was heightened by the imagined response of her peers. Orion could have been reacting to what Labriola (2013) describes as one healthy trigger of jealousy – an instinct to prevent oneself from being disrespected, an aspect which tends to be overshadowed by negative sensations associated with the emotional state.

Ren described how jealousy for her was exacerbated by shame and vulnerability and how she required security in order to feel safe in polyamorous situations.

> Jealousy seems to only come up for me when linked to my primary partner's deep heavy shit and then someone else comes into the dynamic. And shame is usually linked to me as fear of exposure, even if I have major trust with my partner, and that's the big thing if I am going to start sharing deep things with them. Like deep raw parts of me, they need to understand what they can share and what they can't share. If something was in the dynamic that brings things up for me and I get really sad or emotional, knowing that they are going to hold that in a sacred place and not share that with some casual date … Even if I know that my partner is not going to talk about it, there is shame or feeling vulnerable and exposed.

Ren noted that exposing her vulnerability, as people often do with intimate lovers, could place her in an uncomfortable position since her partner may also have other intimate partners. Thus she feared that her personal information would be exposed outside of the couple, bringing up issues of privacy. Although she trusted her partner, there was no guarantee that intimacy would last forever. The emotions of fear, vulnerability, pride, shame, and jealousy were highly intertwined. For Ren, the experience of jealousy was both a vulnerable position to be in and a valuable opportunity to build intimacy through the work they did to alleviate jealousy. Thus, Ren made a connection between vulnerability and intimacy, where jealousy was the vehicle for exploration and personal development.

Ren was among the many of my participants who valued polyamory for its challenges and opportunities for personal growth. Being polyamorous helped Celia take responsibility for her jealousy: "That's actually why I started being poly. Because I am jealous and at one point I needed to not see things as a threat all the time." As shown by the research in Brown's (2012) work on women's shame, intimacy relies on vulnerability. If someone avoids exposing vulnerability, one will simultaneously numb oneself to the possibility of pleasurable emotional experiences, particularly intimate affection. For polyamorists, not only is this vulnerability in relation to a lover's outside relationships, but all intimate relationships have the potential for heartache. Martha described feeling vulnerable with new or potentially casual lovers:

> Fear of getting my heart stomped on. For me, I want to let you in and I want to give you the fullness of this beautiful lovely experience that I'm having with you, but no. Because this is too casual and you are going to stomp all over me and go fuck someone else next week and I'm just a number in a line.

Similarly, Heloise described how she would withhold a degree of intimacy with casual lovers to avoid emotional vulnerability:

> Unless it is a completely non-emotional connection, you are emotionally vulnerable and so you need to know what the emotional vulnerability is with someone who is going to keep it safe. But you don't know that person and it is not a primary relationship. And so you don't actually know that the vulnerability is held by someone who is going to keep it safe.

As described in chapter 3, jealousy holds a unique position for polyamorists: it is at once highly criticized for its roots in compulsory monogamy and also stigmatized since some polyamorists think they should be "over it already." Thus the vulnerability associated with jealousy can be doubled. Alyson noted how hard it was to talk about jealousy sometimes because of the stigma attached to it, both in the mainstream and in polyamorous culture. This was compounded when dating someone who experienced less jealousy or was more sexually active.

> I certainly have my reactions to people and sometimes they are real, sometimes they are imagined and I guess I often, well not often, but I ended up feeling stigmatized because I'm the petty little jealous person and she's very "highly evolved." But the thing we don't talk about that she brings to

the table is years of having the same conversation with people she's having a significant relationship with so really very quickly into it she loses any patience for that conversation and just thinks you are either trying to wreck her good time and so that's the block.

Alyson's account makes apparent the ways in which jealousy, even as it is criticized, can at times retain the dominant culture's view that it is the result of low self-esteem or immaturity. Her statement also demonstrates how jealousy in polyamory is assumed to infringe on a relationship and be a barrier to intimacy.

Coraline challenged polyamory's particular stigmatization of jealousy by being explicit and open about her experience:

My way to deal with it is to talk with other poly people about it. When it comes up and they go "I never feel jealous." I say, "I feel jealous all the time." And they look at me like I've said the total unmentionable. People will be like, "are you having problems?" This is also why people are afraid. I'm like "no, I'm not having a problem, I'm feeling jealous." It's not a problem actually. It's only a problem if you make it a problem. And it is also a problem if you deny it. Any other emotion that you deny gets bigger and bigger and bigger. And it's really interesting because I've only had three distinct experiences where someone brought that up and I automatically responded, and each of the times I was in a group of people who all identified as poly and I said, "Oh, no, I feel jealous all the time" and then the floodgates open and everybody was like, "oh my God ..." and they felt free to actually talk about it, which was really interesting to me and really enforced to me that we are all just making this up as we go along and it's so easy for us to get caught in this posturing of cool poly, right?

Coraline reduced her sense of vulnerability associated with jealousy by naming her experience. By exposing her own experience of jealousy and breaking the silence, Coraline allowed others to feel more at ease to admit their own jealousy. She also pointed to the importance of understanding that emotions are what we make of them, an active creation rather than an external imposition.

Berlant (2006) describes cruel optimism as the attachment we have to objects (or subjects, or even ideology) that causes us to fear its loss. Instead of enjoying the present moment, she argues, we attach to what is not yet lost, or "the condition of maintaining an attachment to a problematic object in advance of its loss" (ibid., 21). In this context, jealousy emerges from a fear of loss coupled with an attachment to the idea of permanence of a relationship. The act of clinging to the attachment, according to Berlant, is what soothes the vulnerability, and thus we indulge in the optimism of the relationship's permanence. As an escape from cruel optimism, Berlant calls for a new mode of relating to our object of desire, which is what many polyamorists are attempting to do. Polyamorists are trying to shift their mode of relating to each other in a way that challenges the assumed necessity of experiencing jealousy in connection to a partner's outside sexual/emotional relations. Poly-amorists retain an emphasis on commitment and thus an assumption that a declaration of love is connected to a future together, but they shift the symbols that represent such commitment, as well as the use of sexual or emotional exclusivity as a tool to bring about commitment or longevity. To do so, some polyamorists embrace vulnerability as a means to access deeper levels of love, without attachment to conventional representations of love.

Limits to Consent

Mistakes are part of the dues that one pays for a full life.

Sophia Loren

One of the overarching goals of polyamorous philosophy and practice is to remove constraining feeling rules, particularly in regard to the mono-normative construction of jealousy as inevitable and intolerable in response to third-party sexual encounters. Within polyamorous phi-losophy, participants aspire to a pure relationship (Giddens 1992), in which each person is able to reach their full potential, without needing each partner to have the same experience in order to equalize power relations. By this philosophy, polyamorists attempt to work with power imbalances that already exist because of the mono-normative culture from which they emerge and to bring them to a mutually supportive balance. However, Klesse (2007) argues that despite the best intentions in these pure relationships, power relations warp the playing field when it comes to negotiating in non-monogamy. Negotiation is central to emotional harmony, and a significant portion of the negotiation in polyamory is done to counteract or prevent instances of jealousy. Opti-mistic guides to polyamory and non-monogamy stress the importance of conflict resolution through "negotiation, self-knowledge and emotion management" (Klesse 2007, 116), but these models can fall short if they do not address deeper power imbalances that may exist even if the relationship is same-sex, polyamorous, queer, or feminist. Those in dominant positions of power, such as those related to race, ethnicity, class, ability, and age, tend to have an upper hand in such negotiations. For example, if one member of the couple wants an open relationship and the other prefers monogamy, the conventional hierarchy of power relations may influence such negotiations. Indeed, there are limits to true agency when negotiating consent and some people consent to agreements that are not their preference.

Klesse's sample includes couples in which only one member wanted to be non-monogamous while the other would have preferred monogamy. By recruiting self-identified polyamorists, my intention was to interview only participants who prefer, or intentionally engage in, polyamorous dynamics. One of the central features of polyamory is the production of consent, with a particular emphasis on honest awareness among the party of lovers and with all choosing to be in the configuration. In theory, if these criteria are not met, actions could border on non-ethical polyamory or even cheating. But consent in sex and polyamory does not always play out simply. In a handful of cases in my sample, there were instances of reluctant or blurry consent or consent granted without full agency.

One poignant example was Tianna, who brought her partner Georgia "kicking and screaming" into polyamory.[20] They were in a long-term and serious relationship, but Tianna described their sex life as "too vanilla," so she wanted another lover with whom she could "fulfil [her] need" to engage in BDSM sexual practices. To Tianna, this was the only reason she wanted to open the relationship. To actualize her BDSM desires, Tianna required not only a sexual but also an emotional connection with a sexual top, but it would otherwise be a secondary relationship, and this was a stipulation of them getting together. My interview was conducted approximately seven years into the relationship between Tianna and Georgia, by which time Georgia had arrived at tolerance but not compersion. Georgia had also on occasion joined in for a threesome (to Tianna's absolute delight). For the bulk of their relationship, Georgia had several lovers of her own, but none became serious, which suited Tianna quite fine. However, Georgia's most recent

---

20   I only spoke with Tianna and not Georgia.

relationship had become serious, which triggered a substantial amount of jealousy for Tianna. After years of working particularly hard to bring herself to a place of tolerance for Tianna's secondary lover, the resentment Georgia faced from Tianna in response to her new lover felt quite unfair. The power relations in this dynamic complicated the ease with which consent in polyamory can sometimes be reached, blurring the lines of both agency and consent. The unspoken power relation at work was that of differing sexual desires and of sexual "inadequacy" (with its likely association with bruised pride).

In polyamorous literature, there is an understanding that certain facets of one's desire should be discussed in advance of a commitment. For example, if one person wants to be monogamous and the other would prefer to have an open relationship, they are likely going to encounter some difficulties. But it is not always the case that such clear negotiations are made when one chooses whom to love. When negotiations take place during this early period of relationships, in the throes of new relationship energy, compromises are made that people may believe at the time are viable. For example, Georgia may have believed and thus agreed to try an open relationship, when her heart (and body) were motivated by NRE, even if on a deeper level she knew it was not ideal for her. Or she may have only agreed to try opening up the relationship in order to maintain her relationship with Tianna. Decisions and commitments made at early stages of a relationship can be influenced by an inflated emotional state. Polyamorists in the NRE stage might believe they are more capable of compersion than they are when the limerence dissipates. Or conversely, some people during this stage may commit to a future of monogamy disproportional to their deeper desires. People make promises (and thus vocally consent) to certain behaviours that they may actually believe temporarily when, as Tianna eloquently stated, "sometimes your dick gets in the way."

Although NRE can be a powerful state, polyamorists recognize that attraction or limerence is not worthy of uprooting one's life. For instance, picture a classic monogamous scenario: a couple have been together for 10 years, have combined their finances, bought a home together, and are raising a family. All is going well, until one day the man (or woman) finds himself (or herself) attracted a person outside the relationship. They begin a flirtatious dynamic and the man feels the spark of the NRE stronger than he has felt for years with his wife. The man interprets the strength of the NRE as love and will then cheat or leave his wife for the new fling, which may or may not have the depth of lasting love. Those versed in consensual non-monogamy will recognize alternatives to the all-or-nothing scenario; potentially they will not assume attraction or infidelity is grounds for divorce but could instead consider that it indicates time for a thorough re-negotiation of priorities, trust, desires, and promises.

In another situation, the unspoken power imbalance was inspired by "lesbian bed death." Martha and her primary partner of three years were in a position where sex had fallen to the wayside. Opening up the relationship was Martha's response to her growing dissatisfaction with their differing sexual desires, and her partner was very reluctant. Thus Martha was exercising a kind of "power of goodbye," indirectly threatening to leave if this "need" was not fulfilled and proposing polyamory to have her sexual needs met outside the relationship, thus enabling them to preserve what was still working in their relationship (emotional intimacy, financial interdependence, cohabitation, etc.). Martha stated,

> We've been talking about poly ever since the beginning of our relation-ship, because I've been a big believer in it … It got to a point where it was all talk and no action and it was only a few weeks ago where I said, that's it! Something needs to happen or I can't stay in this relationship. I just can't. So far it's been like okay, I'll do what I want when I want and I'm checking in with her. And she has her reactions and I have been support-ing her reactions … For the most part it has been a monogamous partner-ship until recently, when I said I'm not doing this anymore. I feel like I'm being repressed. I feel like I'm on a leash and I don't like that. It squishes my spirit and it squishes my life energy.

As in Tianna's scenario, Martha's consideration of polyamory was proposed as a solution to a deficiency in the relationship. Martha had experience with polyamory years prior to this relationship, but she and her current partner had only been monogamous together. While this kind of compartmentalization works on the notion that one person can-not possibly give you everything you need, the emotions involved in a scenario when one is not meeting one's partner's sexual needs are more problematic and intimately tied to power relations. As in Tianna's situ-ation, Martha's primary partner was reluctant to embark on a polyam-orous relationship but was working towards tolerance of the situation likely to please her partner. Again, the power relations involved in this scenario blurred the lines of consent and agency.

Not surprisingly, compersion tends to come more easily for those who feel secure in their relationships and when they feel they have power and control in their relationships. In the two latter scenarios, both Tianna and Martha were in positions of power because they perceived their partners to be in some sense sexually inadequate (or at least incompatible with their current sexual desires). They both expressed a sense of entitlement in feeling that they deserved to get all their needs met inside or outside the relationship. They exercised power in the form of an ultimatum (i.e., you let me do this or I will leave) to secure a reluctant consent. Another interpretation, however, is that they were clearly stating and pursuing their emotional and sexual needs, thus giving their partners full information, which is a significant improvement over the more common action of infidelity or simply ending the relationship.

Orion reported that her past relationships ended primarily because of her attraction to someone outside of the relationship. Thus she was caught in a cycle of serial monogamy where she was repeatedly lying, a dynamic that she found unsatisfying. As a way to break the cycle and avoid infidelity, she pursued an open relationship with her partner Hanna.[21] She was in that relationship for several years, but it had ended shortly before the time of my interview. That partner was reluctant to engage in polyamory but was informed that the alternative was a short-term relationship with Orion that would likely end in her pursuit of someone else. Orion stated that she gave Hanna full knowledge of her history of lying, and Hanna reluctantly agreed to open up their relationship. According to Orion, Hanna was frequently jealous and unhappy with polyamory, and dealing with her jealousy became a burden to Orion. In this scenario, Orion exercised the power of goodbye with difficult and vulnerable honesty (i.e., you have all the information, this is how I come to you, take it or leave it). Their different desires regarding polyamory and monogamy, along with the jealousy that such a dynamic provoked, was the cause of their eventual break-up. Although they were both aware from the beginning of their opposing orientations and of the potential outcome, they pursued the relationship anyway, likely because their short-term desires or chemistry at the beginning of the relationship overrode their long-term plans. Orion's next series of relationships were much more successfully polyamorous (i.e., brought mutual satisfaction), which points to the fact that often learning the

---

21   Again, I only spoke to Orion and not to Hanna.

ropes of polyamory can take time, a few failed attempts, and possibly some broken hearts. Of course, many people also have to try a few monogamous relationships to learn how to make them work. Even with the etiquette and social norms of polyamory, for most participants, it is still a work in progress. As Coraline aptly pointed out, "we are all just making this up as we go along."

Working and Playing with Unequal Power

Nothing ever goes away until it teaches us what we need to know.
Pema Chodron

Like many queer and feminist activists, polyamorists often formulate relationships that work with unequal power structures instead of trying to impose sameness. Instead of enforcing parallels, they attempt to address the outcome of power differentials by easing emotional troubles. Polyamorists find creative ways to work and play with the intensity of jealousy, on both emotional and erotic levels.

The ways in which my participants responded to differences in power were varied. Many found more interesting ways to compromise than to default to the lowest common denominator. For example, if one person had another partner and the other person did not, the couple did not require one to get rid of their partner or force the other to acquire a partner. Instead, they worked with this difference and focused on trying to bring about a feeling of compersion in both partners. If there were no "hard feelings" then the "power difference" was not an impediment (or, potentially, not even a power difference). Courtney identified power this way: "We are not talking about play power, we are talking about actual angst imbalance in the relationship." My participants did not require that each partner spend the same amount of time with each lover, but rather tried to minimize challenging emotions so that this did not matter. In other words, sameness was not necessary to balance power. To counter the power of jealousy, some participants tried to work through the suffering they experienced rather than attempting to avoid it. Thus, avoiding potentially jealousy-provoking situations was not the only way to attain compersion (nor was it necessarily an effective option); working through the challenging emotion appeared to be a more successful route for many polyamorists.

Lupton (1998, 71) identifies

> [two] notions of emotion that are circulating today ... The first is a prod-
> uct of the negative discourses on emotion that position it as dangerous,
> disruptive or humiliating, and portray emotionality as evidence of lack
> of self-control. The second is the contrasting positive discourses on emo-
> tion that represent it as authentic evidence of humanity, selfhood and the
> proper basis of judgment and morality.

In my study, both of these notions came into play with regard to jealousy. Jealousy was at once seen as shameful, disruptive, uncontrolled,
or rampant, while at the same time it was also described as an authentic
and legitimate part of sexual and intimate relationships. Notably, both
negative and positive emotional discourses can be judged in reverse.
For example, even love or ecstatic joy can be perceived as turning one
into a naive fool. The lack of passion and disinterestedness that typifies
"coolness" is frequently glorified.

Polyamorous theory re-evaluates conventional notions of love, in
particular sexual exclusivity as representative of love or commitment.
Polyamorists aspire to a version of confluent love, which Giddens (1992,
61) describes as "active, contingent love, and therefore jars with the 'forever,' 'one-and-only,' qualities of the romantic love complex." Further,
Giddens argues that sexual exclusivity is not what holds confluent love
together. Rather, it is the "acceptance on the part of each partner, 'until
further notice,' that each gains sufficient benefit from the relation to
make its continuance worthwhile" (ibid., 63). Brown (2000, 39) argues,

> Although confluent love (as an ideal type of love) tells us what we should
> do with our feelings (disclose them, open them up), it is dependent upon
> the idea that our capacity for rational decision making can overcome irra-
> tional obstructions with increased levels of self-reflexivity.

Self-reflective disclosure is a central means by which polyamorists re-
craft emotional scripts. Self-reflexivity is commonly achieved through
communication with one's partner(s), often with the intention of identifying and negotiating preferences or working through power imbalances to cultivate compersion. Although they noted the difficulty of this
work, many of my participants celebrated the challenge and the ensuing rewards that came as a result of it. Power was rarely equalized, but
the dynamics in the relationship were brought to a place of emotional
fulfilment and compersion. Thus, the equality sought in confluent love
was mediated through compersion, not sameness.

To many participants, the emotional challenge of polyamorous practice was beneficial because it was understood as a good place to learn, grow, and develop oneself. Some polyamorists even pursued polyamory because of the challenges it obliged practitioners to confront. Coraline valued the lessons learned through practising polyamory:

> If you want to just stand in one place and not move, don't choose poly. Because the ground has shifted all the time. It's moving all the time … Poly doesn't make you a better or a worse person but it sure makes you ask those questions about yourself. And I really love that aspect of it. Sometimes I find it exhausting, but when I find it exhausting I just step off for a while.

Though she welcomed the challenges that accompany polyamory, Coraline was also willing to acknowledge and choose when to take on those challenges. Ren was particularly forthright in welcoming polyamory's challenges. For her, jealousy in polyamory as well as sexual relationships in general were ideal places to locate and work through personal issues:

> For me jealousy is just a barometer to show my own issues, like what I have to work on. Like if I am jealous, I have to assess why that is happening. It's never someone else's fault … I like my sexual relationships to be a place where I work through stuff. Like I use kink as a tool to work through emotional stuff … because I want to live wide open, I prefer to have relationships that are really raw and emotional and big and for a purpose.

Power in polyamory is entangled in dynamics that link pleasure and pain, compersion and jealousy, challenge and growth. Power relations manifest not only in relation to sexuality but also materially in regard to economic and financial matters, which can translate into jealousy or envy. Financial power is certainly relevant in monogamous arrangements; in polyamorous dynamics, financial power is complicated by the number of partners sharing resources.[22] Fidelity occurs not only in emotional or sexual circumstances, but in many other ways, including financially. In a discussion about trust in relationships, Rihanna offered an example of financial infidelity:

---

22   Other material manifestations of power further complicated by the multiple relationships in polyamory not addressed in detail here include child-care duties, parental care, disabilities, health care, and housework.

There still needs some sort of emotional support base because there are lots of types of infidelity. There is certainly the sexual infidelity and a lot of people will give sexual infidelity a total pass, as long as safety is maintained, but can't handle emotional infidelity. And then there's other people who are okay with some of the others, but are not into financial infidelity … [I can handle] "don't ask don't tell" about sex, but [not] financial infidelity … That's another way that people can be unfaithful and another object of jealousy can be money.

It is interesting that there is no term for a financial threat to a relationship, in comparison to jealousy as a term for a sexual/emotional threat to a relationship. Heloise described how she minimized financial power differences between her and her wife, who was a stay-at-home parent, in a way that was likely not much different from what may be done in a monogamous relationship:

At this time I feel like I really know that we will be together for the rest of our lives. And yet I take what I think are appropriate steps just in case we are not, like I want Priscilla to have her own credit card, because she is the one at home. I bought her a diamond ring so she has something to sell if I kick her to the curb. [*laughter*] I'm joking, but I'm not.

Another interesting way in which polyamorists work with power differences is through their acceptance of "double standards." Instead of equalizing power by making everyone's experience the same, polyamorists find ways to work with multiple, differing desires. Rihanna talked about having a relationship, which she called "mono-poly," in which she had other lovers, but her boyfriend did not. He preferred to be a secondary lover to her and did not want to have other lovers. Similarly, Alex had two steady long-term partners, one who had many other casual lovers, and the other who was not currently dating anyone else. According to Alex, all members of this poly configuration were satisfied with their situation. Francine had one primary and one secondary girlfriend, neither of whom had other lovers, and according to her, both were satisfied with their status in the primary/secondary hierarchy. She also stated that they were all open to changing the configuration in the future as the opportunity arose. Such double standards are at once simple and yet highly innovative and involve self-reflection on the deeper intentions of one's polyamorous practice. Francine described how in her approach to polyamory, she focused on relinquishing control:

So many things are not within our control and we have this desire to control it. To me there is something very empowering about letting go. Honestly, what does control get you? Does it get you a real authentic experience? Not really. Because if you are busy controlling something, you're actually busy manipulating it and it's not what it would be if you just let it be. It's like in martial arts; it's all about self-control, it's not about external control. Martial arts in its true form is not about aggressing on someone else. It's about redirecting their own physicality. They punch at you, you turn that punch back. It's about them receiving their own punch.

In this statement, Francine demonstrated how she worked with difficult experiences of jealousy rather than trying to avoid them in order to live a lifestyle that better suited her desires. As Francine's martial art metaphor makes clear, polyamorists can take the power in jealousy and redirect this energy into positive emotional experiences, into compersion, or into sexual energy.

As further demonstrated in Francine's narrative, jealousy and power overlap in regard to matters of control. Some people express jealousy as an attempt to control the actions of another person, as a way to regain a sense of control over their partner's actions, how they feel or their life outside a relationship. Some polyamorists are drawn to this lifestyle for the challenge of overcoming this need to control. Rihanna described her experience of compersion in the following way: "Instead of a clutching at the heart where it's closing in, it's more like it's opening up." Rihanna described a sense of caring without trying to control someone or the parameters of the relationship, having a sense of peace and security from a relationship. Relinquishing control can be a matter of vulnerability. Opening up a relationship can indeed be risky to one's heart. A common sentiment among my participants pointed to the importance of allowing oneself to be vulnerable in order to inspire more intimacy in connections. This challenge of overcoming emotional constraints, along with its ensuing reward, was itself a motivation for many of my participants to pursue polyamory.

Some polyamorists used the terms "non-possessiveness" or "loving non-attachment" to describe their attempts to love unconditionally while encouraging their partner(s) to live authentically and express full freedom. Polyamory requires a kind of letting go of one's hold over a lover's actions. Many of my participants found this to be a vulnerable yet gratifying position. Some were initially fearful about allowing a lover to explore their sexuality outside the relationship (fear of loss, fear of a preference for the other person, etc.), yet for many, once they delved into it, the fear vanished and the power it had over them in terms of jealousy dissipated.

Playing with Power

To truly laugh, you must be able to take your pain and play with it.

Charlie Chaplin

De Visser and McDonald's (2007, 473) study found that "rather than seeking to eliminate jealousy, swingers may manage their jealousy in order to increase sexual excitement and arousal." Similarly, some polyamorists in my study found ways to play with the erotically charged emotion of jealousy that increased overall libido. In the following quotation Ren described how her partner's sexual encounters increased her sexual energy:

> I've found that if I'm not feeling very sexual and my lover goes out, because they are feeling fulfilled and wanted, I want to get close to that again. Even if I wasn't feeling [it before], like I am having a hard winter and all of a sudden my partner comes home smelling like pheromones with a smile on their face and they are like "I'm going to make you breakfast in bed." They are energized by that. They feel hot. The world looks sparkly. They're feeling good. Then I'm like, oh yeah. That feels good. I want to get closer to it. It's magnetic. It keeps on coming.

This statement reveals a positive unintended consequence of increased sexual feelings that arise from compersion.

My study revealed that in addition to experiencing increased libido, some polyamorists eroticized and played with the emotional intensity of jealousy rather than converting that emotion into compersion. Though this may be considered a kind of compersion, it still retained a sensation of jealousy, an erotically charged pain rather than joy. This kind of power conversion parallels a sadomasochistic practice where sexual power is intentionally exaggerated and played with, shifting the negativity of power differentials (Califia 1994), and thus it may be called emotional masochism or a kind of erotic anguish. Heloise recounted the following story after our interview was interrupted by a personalized ringtone from her wife that played the song "Banging on the Bathroom Floor" (by Shaggy).

It's a song about cheating. It's not a song about monogamy, it's a song about cheating. Priscilla and I have this whole fantasy about cheating. Well okay, this is how it started. I was like, "wouldn't it be so hot if you took an ad out in the paper?" Because she's at home while I'm working, this was before we had kids and she was home. You put out an ad, "Housewife at home, looking for someone totally discreet. My wife is at work. Come on over." You have a few dates, then one day I come home, and it serves her right. She's helping someone cheat on their partner. I come home and I catch them in bed and I go into a jealous rage. She'd run off and we'd have mad passionate sex because it would be so kinky … I would love to go into a jealous rage, that would be totally hot! [*laughter*]

Heloise's narrative demonstrates the ways that she and her wife eroticized and played with jealousy. For ethical reasons, they decided to keep this scenario as a fantasy rather than actualize it.

Leigh argued that "possession and ownership is absolutely eroticized in our relationship. Absolutely." Similarly, Ren found a way to sexualize jealousy:

Jealousy can also be hot if you flip it. If you play with that and you know that ultimately you are taken care of and if you are like okay this doesn't feel good anymore so everyone stops. But like, I'm going to tie you up while I make out with this person in front of you. "Aren't you jealous? You want to be here. You wish this but it's totally making you super hot." Like that, I like a lot … As long as it's safe, jealousy can spark hotness. Possession and playing with the idea that I own you and that you're mine, like oh, "that person may have gotten a taste of you but [*whispered*] you're mine." That's a fun thing to feel because you can be held, it's like being restrained. I'm going to put you in shackles because I hold you and you're safe. So I'm going to possess you. You are mine. I may permit you to be around other people or whatever. Playing with that is good.

Ren's exhibitionistic/voyeuristic arousal demonstrates the complicated connection between jealousy, power, and arousal.

Also noteworthy in these interview extracts is how jealousy is not simplistically negative; it can also inspire positive feelings that are distinct from compersion. There may be moments that are singularly pleasurable or painful, but there are also moments of a complex array of mixed emotions. Negotiation or processing might require emotional labour, patience, and vulnerability, yet these may also be joyful moments and inspire particular satisfaction. Indeed, certain people quite enjoy processing in relationships, and some people even extend the time in which they engage in discussions of their emotions, which in some circumstances may display as manufacturing "drama." Another example of mixed emotion is that of melancholy, experiencing a kind of pleasure in wallowing in sadness. Melancholy is one reason people enjoy listening to sad music or linger in their sadness instead of immediately trying to return to happiness. Indeed, many people take comfort in melancholic sadness. The practice of polyamory, and relationships in general, enables experiences that break the simplistic dichotomy between good and bad emotions, as well as the division between work and play.

Conclusion

Jealousy is invariably caught in a complex web of power relations. Polyamory is a marginal sexual practice subject to formal and informal regulations. In this chapter, I set out to understand how polyamorists rethink power relations in their interpersonal relationships as well as in response to institutional mono-normativity. I found instances where polyamorists both resisted and reproduced dominant power structures. For example, negotiations were at times done with attention to the emotional needs of all parties involved. Other times people reproduced dominant power structures with manipulative versions of "consent." My participants sometimes achieved compersion as a form of resistance to mono-normativity, and in other instances, jealousy was the painful outcome. At times, polyamorists devised creative ways to work with power imbalances; other times, the dominant paradigm was replicated in their relationships.

Because "sexual acts are burdened with an excess of significance" (Rubin 1993, 11), having more than one lover remains culturally challenging. Polyamorous relationships are not necessarily a form of resistance to dominant power structures. And, as noted by the copious accounts of polyagony, not all polyamorous practice leads to compersion or to embodied pleasure. However, working (and play-ing) with the emotional challenges that are seemingly inherent to polyamorous practice can lead to greater intimacy, self-assuredness, and personal strength. For polyamorists, resistance to dominant relationship models often starts from a place of self-care and prizes emotional acts of pleasure.

After reading and analysing hundreds of transcript pages of accounts of polyamory and polyagony, I believe that polyamorous practice indeed requires a great deal of courage. Polyamory can have significant rewards, but the work required to achieve such success is no small feat. Polyamorists overcome jealousy, personal challenges, and social criticism, as well as internalized polyphobia. Polyamorists require courage to open their hearts to vulnerable emotions, to resist conventions, and to live out a marginalized lifestyle. I commend my participants for their courageous efforts and thank them greatly for their willingness to share their stories with me.

6 Polyamory's Legacy: Concluding Remarks

A re-imagined polyamory could successfully transform systemic inequalities in hegemonic social structures by focusing on addressing common issues in relationships and families as well as by developing norms of inclusivity. Such systemic inequalities include those connected with gender and sexuality.

Melita Noël

Jealousy is at once common and complicated. Throughout this book, I have attempted to enrich conventional understandings of this very common emotion and also make comprehensible this particularly complex emotional experience. Polyamorists face an interesting dilemma: in a monogamy-centric culture, any act or desire for extra-relationship encounters is expected to be met with the inevitable and intolerable experience of jealousy. Jealousy is thought to be a sign of love, and thus a partner's jealousy is interpreted as evidence of commitment to the relationship. Polyamorists intentionally engage in sexual and emotional relationships with multiple people and create their own cultural norms with the intention of minimizing instances of jealousy and enabling compersion in its stead. Jealousy, for polyamorists, is seen as a barrier to love and to romantic pursuits. Pursuing other relationships is not considered reason enough for a partner to be jealous and a partner's jealousy is not considered a reason in and of itself to halt the pursuit of other relationships.

Among my participants' accounts, I encountered vibrant stories of successfully compersive polyamory, yet in other instances, some of them replicated the dominant cultural norms they were trying to escape. For example, some of my participants argued that jealousy was irrelevant in a particular circumstance but then found jealousy's grip inescapable. They would reflect upon their desires, negotiate with the best intentions, and still encounter polyagonous results. This tension between intentions and outcomes was apparent throughout my analysis. As one participant, Coraline, noted, "we are all trying to figure it out as we go along." Although non-monogamy has a long history in practice, polyamorists have often been disconnected from this history and seem to reinvent the wheel every few generations. As polyamory gains momentum, as well as mainstream attention, I suspect some of the tensions that result from mono-normativity will be minimized. And the polyamorous influence on mono-normativity and on conventional understandings of jealousy could be profound. As Noël described in the epigraph of this chapter, polyamory has transformative potential for systemic power inequalities.

In response to my quest to find the intersection between what polyamorists are doing and what they wish they were doing, it seems as though there is an iterative dance between theory and practice. The theory developed by polyamorists is progressing to better match actual emotional interactions, and as discourse develops, polyamorists are increasingly personalizing their relational practices outside of either monogamous or polyamorous directives. While only practised by a small minority, polyamory and its philosophy are gaining popular attention and a degree of mainstream credibility (Mint 2007b), such that the sociocultural dimension of polyamory is beginning to reverberate outside the polyamorous community. To understand the actual and potential influence of the culture of polyamory on monogamy, on mono-normativity, and on conventional understandings of jealousy, I find it useful to draw on McLuhan and McLuhan's (1988) model of technological reverberations, asking how a new social idea makes other ideas obsolete, retrieves/renews others, enhances/remixes others, and reverses previously available concepts. In this sense, polyamory is a sociocultural idea, or a "relational understanding" (Haritaworn, Lin, and Klesse 2006, 518) of society that has the potential to transform social practices. Polyamory exerts all four effects not only on the polyamorous community but also on dominant cultural conceptualizations of monogamy and jealousy. Ideas themselves can spur social change.

Polyamory will never make monogamy obsolete, but what makes the practice and sociocultural construction of polyamory potentially profound are the ways in which polyamory problematizes and challenges whole sets of stagnant social norms that are taken for granted in a mono-normative culture. Polyamorists break the silence and stigma attached to non-monogamy. Polyamory challenges the gender stereotype that women are naturally monogamous and men naturally inclined towards non-monogamy, and thus the idea that only men would want to have multiple partners. In Western culture, men are subjected to an interplay of competing archetypes of manhood. On the one hand, men are scolded for engaging in or even wanting extramarital affairs, but men's masculinity can also be called into question if they do not want multiple partners. Women's desire for non-monogamy is usually met with disproportionate scorn and regulation (Ryan and Jetha 2010). As this belief is challenged, ideas about the way men and women should act are subsequently changing.

Polyamory shifts the notion that jealousy is the inevitable and intolerable outcome of one's partner having sex or relationships with other people. Polyamory helps reveal the socially constructed link between the mono-normative model of love and conventions of jealousy and challenges the seeming "naturalness" of these assumptions. Polyamorists are trying to make obsolete the notion that jealousy should be used as a tool for manipulation or control (as is often portrayed in dominant media), such as the use of jealousy to attract attention from a partner. Polyamorists also challenge the concept that it is prudent to be flattered by a partner's jealousy and the idea that a partner's jealousy is indicative of their love and commitment to the relationship or, conversely, that a lack of jealousy is characteristic of a commitment deficiency.

Polyamory also inspires the retrieval of knowledge concerning non-monogamy. For example, non-monogamy was part of a thriving dialogue in the 1970s among lesbians but went out of fashion during the 1980s partly in reaction to HIV/AIDS and its subsequent link to promiscuity (Munson and Stelboum 1999; Klesse 2006a), though it was also due in part to shifting feminist politics (particularly the feminist "sex wars" which associated non-monogamy with promiscuity and hence with patriarchy; see Vance 1989). Non-monogamy is having a cultural and academic renaissance (Barker and Langdridge 2010a), a result of the convergence of political dialogues and emergence of the Internet as a means to connect. Polyamory has led to the retrieval of knowledge of earlier forms of consensual non-monogamy, for example publications of historical practices (Anderlini-D'Onofrio 2009) and scientific research on the evidence of prehistoric non-monogamy and non-monogamy in the animal world (Ryan and Jetha 2010). Arguably, these ideas were never "lost," but their greater awareness in Western culture and peer-reviewed scholarship is a form of retrieval.

In regard to how polyamory can enhance/remix social life, much of polyamorous discourse and activism is aimed at enhancing the communication skills and romantic/sexual experiences of polyamorists. Polyamorous discourse and activism also increases the number and kind of relationship choices available. Whereas people in the past may have practised monogamy as the only possible option, and thus potentially fallen into serial monogamy or cheated, polyamory offers another option. More options do not necessarily lead to enhancement of social life, what Schwartz (2004) calls "the paradox of choice." However, greater societal awareness of polyamory means that those who find they desire non-monogamy have, at the very least, an expansive vocabulary with which to describe their desires and, arguably, are better able to act upon them. Polyamorists sometimes assert that denying outside attractions (especially if they are taboo) often leads to increased desire and infatuation, whereas communicating about them could minimize suspicious jealousy since all the factors are known. People may make better choices or select more compatible partners if their attraction tendencies or relationship style preference (monogamy, polyamory, swinging, etc.) is up front and less socially stigmatized.

Polyamory is still a relatively new idea in many social circles, but in communities that are receptive, it is often perceived as a progressive or "evolved" way of having relationships. Within some queer communities, polyamory is increasingly becoming the new chic and some people actually feel pressure to be poly. Thus, within these small pockets, this transvaluation of values, or McLuhanian reversal, can at times have a negative pressuring effect. Original publications on polyamory were written with a rose-tinted gloss and slight defensiveness to guard against criticism of the practice, and thus they often came out as having celebratory tone (see Klesse 2006a). Now that the discourse has been developing for well over a decade, there is more nuanced critical analysis of the practice, accounting for the various highs and lows, ambitions and shortcomings, resistance and reproduction. We see fewer mutually exclusive splits and cultural distancing between polyamory and monogamy, swinging, and even polyshagory. The fluid movement between identities, practices, and communities has more acceptability.

I opened my book by presenting the two most common responses I receive when I bring up the subject of polyamory: questions regarding jealousy and time. My sense is that these questions about polyamory are really concerned with the viability of loving more than one person and sustaining such relationships. The question of viability is confounded by society's conception of romantic love. Feminists have been apt to "deconstruct and deride" romantic love (Brown 2006, 3), and theorists continue to philosophize what qualifies as love, yet as Jackson (1993) notes, "even sociologists fall in love." Even as we critique the social construction of relationship structures, we can still be joyfully swept away by the delightful tug of attraction or overwhelmed by the sadness that accompanies its loss. There is indeed a discrepancy between the theoretical critique of romantic ideology and the embodied desire when one is in the midst of a romantic affair. Polyamory could be seen as the epitome of the romantic ideal since polyamorists sustain multiple long-term romantic relationships, or it could be interpreted as a departure from such an ideology since it defies the central tenet of romantic ideology – i.e., sexual exclusivity. Still, the experience of jealousy comes in to complicate the experience of love.

My intention with this study is neither to make any claims about polyamory's viability as a whole nor to make claims about individuals' ability to be polyamorous or compersive. Instead, my intention throughout this book has been to examine the feeling rules associated with the emotion world in which mono-normativity operates and to explore how polyamorists rethink and reconstruct their own set of feeling rules. With the introduction of word "compersion" into the polyamorist repertoire comes the hope that polyamorists will be more apt to experience such pleasure. While emotions tend to be experienced as internal, private affairs, they indeed emerge through the co-constitutive interaction between the individual and their society. As such, emotional experiences and expressions that are scripted by our emotion worlds can also be reworked through subcultural practices or deliberate training. Although polyamorous philosophies are well developed, the pursued emotional experiences did not always correspond. And yet, to many polyamorists, the compersive benefit, emotional growth, and, to be candid, general delight that ensued from their polyamorous practice was gratifying and indeed worth the effort.

When discussing polyamory, I am often confronted with "but what if" statements. People ask me, "But what if your lover does leave you for their new lover?" "But what if you do like her better?" "But what if you just don't have the time to maintain the relationship and all the processing it requires?" Polyamorists often reply to these statements with comparisons to monogamy or examples of times when polyamory is successful. For example, "the chances are just as high for a lover to leave if the relationship is monogamous." "They are more likely to stay with me because of the freedom afforded to polyamory than if they are limited by the confines of monogamy." "The risk of them liking the other person more is more likely if the situation is left taboo." "I can make the time to pick up a new hobby like aerial dancing or to incorporate a new friend into my life, so I can also make the time for another relationship."

That said, among the array of stories I heard from my interviewees and from the larger polyamorous community, there were circumstances when the "but what if" scenarios were actualized. For example, one polyamorist left her primary lover to settle down in a monogamous arrangement, and another polyamorist broke up with her secondary lover because she did not have the time to give to her primary lover. I have heard several accounts of people who were non-monogamous in their younger years until they met the "love of their lives" with whom they settled down.

Instances of polyagony should not be used to challenge the viability of polyamory as a whole. When monogamous relationships break down because of infidelity, replacements, or boredom (which are monogamy's most common "but what if" equivalents), people do not generally blame monogamy for the relationship's demise (with the exception of Ryan and Jetha 2010, who do precisely this). Thus my interest is directed at the intersection of individuals' experiences in relationships, social institutions, and power structures. Importantly, sexuality is fluid and people fluctuate in their sexual expression (see Diamond 2008). For many people, polyamory is a temporary phase – something to try out for its excitement, its sexual charge, and the variety it offers. For other people, polyamory is a long-term commitment, identity, or practice. Whether their practice was a temporary experiment or a life-long arrangement, for my participants polyamory had many benefits and seemed to be a vibrant addition to their romantic, sexual, and emotional lives, and I do extrapolate such benefits to many other polyamorists.

Opening one's heart to the vulnerability of open relationships means counteracting dominant ideas and power structures that can be deeply embedded in one's emotional make-up, an experience which may be as challenging as it is rewarding. And consequently, the more one opens up their heart to polyamorous possibilities, the more one may be able to conquer love's jealous shadow. With the knowledge that love requires vulnerability, which requires great courage, let me leave you with a quote from Anais Nin, who has profoundly inspired me as I continue to explore my own polyamorous practice and research:

Life shrinks or expands in proportion to one's courage.

Works Cited

Adam, B. (2006). Relationship innovation in male couples. *Sexualities*, 9(1), 5–26.

Ahmed, S. (2004a). Collective feelings: Or, the impression left by others. *Theory, Culture & Society*, 21(2), 25–42.

Ahmed, S. (2004b). *The cultural politics of emotion*. Edinburgh: Edinburgh University Press.

Ahmed, S. (2012). Sociable happiness. In D. Spencer, K. Walby, and A. Hunt (Eds.), *Emotions matter: A relational approach to emotions* (pp. 40–62). Toronto: University of Toronto Press.

Anderlini-D'Onofrio, S. (Ed.). (2004). *Plural loves: Designs for bi and poly living*. Binghamton, NY: The Haworth Press.

Anderlini-D'Onofrio, S. (2009). *Gaia and the new politics of love: Notes for a poly planet*. Berkeley, CA: North Atlantic Books.

Barash, S.S. (2006). *Tripping the prom queen: The truth about women and rivalry*. New York: St Martin's Press.

Barbalet, J. (1998). *Emotion, social theory and social structure: A macrosociological approach*. Cambridge: Cambridge University Press.

Barker, M. (2005). This is my partner, and this is my … partner's partner: Constructing a polyamorous identity in a monogamous world. *Journal of Constructivist Psychology*, 18(1), 75–88.

Barker, M., and Langdridge, D. (Eds.). (2010a). *Understanding non-monogamies*. New York: Routledge.

Barker, M., and Langdridge, D. (2010b). Whatever happened to non-monogamies? Critical reflections on recent research and theory. *Sexualities*, 13(6), 748–72.

Barker, M., and Ritchie, A. (2007). Hot bi babes and feminist families: Polyamorous women speak out. *Lesbian & Gay Psychology Review*, 8(2), 141–51.

Baumeister, R.F. (2000). Gender differences in erotic plasticity: The female drive as socially flexible and responsive. *Psychological Bulletin*, 126(3), 347–74.

Baumgart, H. (1990). *Jealousy: Experiences and solutions*. Chicago: University of Chicago Press.

Ben-Ze'ev, A., and Goussinsky, R. (2008). *In the name of love: Romantic ideology and its victims*. New York: Oxford University Press.

Berlant, L. (2006). Cruel optimism: Optimism and its objects. *Differences: A Journal of Feminist Cultural Studies, 17*(3), 20–36.

Bersani, L. (1995). *Homos*. Cambridge, MA: Harvard University Press.

Boler, M. (1999). *Feeling power: Emotions and education*. New York: Routledge.

Bronski, M. (1998). *The pleasure principle: Sex, backlash and the struggle for gay freedom*. New York: St Martin's Press.

Brown, B. (2012). *Daring greatly: How the courage to be vulnerable transforms the way we live, love, parent and lead*. New York: Gotham Books.

Brown, J. (2000). What is a psychoanalytic sociology of emotion? *Psychoanalytic Studies, 2*(1), 35–49.

Brown, J. (2006). *A psychosocial exploration of love and intimacy*. Houndmills, UK: Palgrave Macmillan.

Bryson, J. (1991). Modes of response to jealousy evoking situations. In P. Salovey (Ed.), *The psychology of jealousy and envy* (pp. 178–205). New York: Guilford Press.

Buss, D. (2000). *The dangerous passion: Why jealousy is as necessary as love or sex*. London: Bloomsbury.

Butler, J. (1990). *Gender trouble: Feminism and the subversion of identity*. New York: Routledge.

Califia, P. (1994). *Public sex: The culture of radical sex*. San Francisco: Cleis Press.

Cardoso, D., Correia, C., and Capella, D. (2009). Polyamory as a possibility of feminine empowerment. European Sociological Association Abstract Book. Retrieved from http://esa.abstractbook.net/abstract.php?aID=4901

Carpenter, C.J. (2012). Meta-analysis of sex differences in responses to sexual versus emotional infidelity: Men and women are more similar than different. *Psychology of Women Quarterly, 36*, 24–37.

Clanton, G. (1996). A sociology of jealousy. *International Journal of Sociology and Social Policy, 16*(9–10), 171–89.

Clanton, G. (2001). Jealousy in American culture, 1945–1985. In A. Branaman (Ed.), *Self in society: Blackwell readers in sociology* (pp. 156–66). Malden: Blackwell.

Clanton, G., and Smith, L. (1977). *Jealousy*. Upper Saddle River, NJ: Prentice Hall.

Clough, P., and Halley, J. (Eds.). (2007). *The affective turn: Theorizing the social*. Durham, NC: Duke University Press.

De Visser, R., and McDonald, D. (2007). Swings and roundabouts: Management of jealousy in heterosexual "swinging" couples. *British Journal of Psychology, 46*, 459–76.

Diamond, L. (2008). *Sexual fluidity: Understanding women's love and desire.* Cambridge, MA: Harvard University Press.

Duncombe, J., Harrison, K., Allan, G., and Marsden, D. (2004). *The state of affairs: Explorations in infidelity and commitment.* Hillsdale, NJ: Lawrence Erlbaum.

Easton, D., and Liszt, C.A. (1997). *The ethical slut: A guide to infinite sexual possibilities.* Emeryville, CA: Greenery Press.

Ebin, J. (2006). Developing successful sexual health and support services for bisexual people: Lessons learned from the BiHealth Program. *Journal of Bisexuality, 6*(102), 165–89.

Edalati, A., and Redzuan, M. (2010). The relationship between jealousy and aggression: A review of literatures related to wives' aggression. *European Journal of Scientific Research, 39*(4), 498–504.

Fausto-Sterling, A. (2000). *Sexing the body: Gender politics and the construction of sexuality.* New York: Basic Books.

Ferrer, J. (2007). Monogamy, polyamory and beyond. *Tikkun, 22*(1), 37–62.

Fine, C. (2010). *Delusions of gender: The real science behind sex differences.* New York: Norton.

Francis, E. (n.d.). Compassion and Compersion. http://www.ericfrancis.com/scorpio/scorpio22.html

Giddens, A. (1992). *The transformation of intimacy: Sexuality, love, and eroticism in modern societies.* Stanford, CA: Stanford University Press.

Gould, T. (1999). *The lifestyle: A look at the erotic rites of swingers.* Toronto: Vintage Canada.

Grosz, E. (1994). *Volatile bodies: Towards a corporeal feminism.* Bloomington: Indiana University Press.

Guerrero, L., Trost, M., and Yoshimura, S. (2005). Romantic jealousy: Emotions and communicative responses. *Personal Relationships, 12*: 233–52.

Halberstam, J. (1998). *Female masculinity.* Durham, NC: Duke University Press.

Halperin, D. (1995). *Saint Foucault: Towards a gay hagiography.* New York: Oxford University Press.

Hankivsky, O. (2011). *Health inequities in Canada: Intersectional frameworks and practices.* Vancouver: UBC Press.

Harding, J., and Pribram, E.D. (2002). The power of feeling: Locating emotions in culture. *European Journal of Cultural Studies, 5*(4), 407–26.

Harding, J., and Pribram, E.D. (2004). Losing our cool: Following Williams and Grossberg on emotions. *Cultural Studies, 18*(6), 863–83.

Haritaworn, J., Lin, C.J., and Klesse, C. (2006). Poly/logue: A critical introduction to polyamory. *Sexualities, 9*(5), 515–29.

Hart, S., and Legerstee, M. (Eds.). (2010). *Handbook of jealousy: Theory, research and multidisciplinary approaches.* Hoboken, NJ: Wiley-Blackwell.

Heaphy, B., Donovan, C., and Weeks, J. (2004). A different affair? Openness and nonmonogamy in same sex relationships. In J. Duncombe, K. Harrison, G. Allan, and D. Marsden (Eds.), *The state of affairs: Explorations in infidelity and commitment* (pp. 167–86). Hillsdale, NJ: Lawrence Erlbaum.

Hill Collins, P. (2000). *Black feminist thought: Knowledge, consciousness, and the politics of empowerment.* New York: Routledge.

Hochschild, A. (1979). Emotion work, feeling rules and social structure. *American Journal of Sociology, 85,* 551–75.

Hupka, R., and Ryan, J. (1990). The cultural contribution to jealousy: Cross-cultural aggression in sexual jealousy situations. *Cross-Cultural Research, 24*(1–4), 51–71.

Iantaffi, A. (2010). Disability and polyamory: Exploring the edges of interdependence, gender and queer issues in non-monogamous relationships. In M. Barker and T. Langdridge (Eds.), *Understanding non-monogamies* (pp. 160–8). New York: Routledge.

Jackson, S. (1993). Even sociologists fall in love: An exploration in the sociology of emotions. *Sociology, 27*(2), 201–20.

Jaggar, A. (1989). Love and knowledge: Emotion in feminist epistemology. *Inquiry, 32,* 151–76.

Jamieson, L. (2004). Intimacy, negotiated nonmonogamy and the limits of the couple. In J. Duncombe, K. Harrison, G. Allan, and D. Marsden (Eds.), *The state of affairs: Explorations in infidelity and commitment* (pp. 31–52). Hillsdale, NJ: Lawrence Erlbaum.

Jordan-Young, R. (2010). *Brainstorm: The flaw in science and sex differences.* Cambridge, MA: Presidents and Fellows of Harvard University.

Katz, J. (2012). Emotion's crucible. In D. Spencer, K. Walby, and A. Hunt (Eds.), *Emotions matter: A relational approach to emotions* (pp. 15–39). Toronto: University of Toronto Press.

Kemper, T. (2008). Power, status, and emotions. In M. Greco and P. Stenner (Eds.), *Emotions: A social science reader* (pp. 127–31). London: Routledge.

Kenney, J.S., and Craig, A. (2012). Illegitimate pain: Introducing a concept and a research agenda. In D. Spencer, K. Walby, and A. Hunt (Eds.), *Emotions matter: A relational approach to emotions* (pp. 86–101). Toronto: University of Toronto Press.

Kipnis, L. (2004). *Against love: A polemic.* Toronto: Vintage Press.

Klein, M. (1997). *Envy and Gratitude and other works: 1946–1963.* London: Vintage Press.

Klesse, C. (2006a). Polyamory and its "others": Contesting the terms of non-monogamy. *Sexualities, 9*(5), 565–83.

Klesse, C. (2006b). The trials and tribulations of being a "slut": Ethical, psychological and political thoughts on polyamory. Christian Klesse in conversation with Dossie Easton. *Sexualities, 9*(5), 643–50.

Klesse, C. (2007). *The spectre of promiscuity: Gay male and bisexual non-monogamies and polyamories.* Burlington: Ashgate.

La Rochefoucauld, F.D. (1967). *Reflections: Or, sentences and moral maxims.* London: Penguin Books.

Labriola, K. (2013). *The jealousy workbook: Exercises and insights for managing open relationships.* Emeryville, CA: Greenery Press.

Lazarus, R. (1991). *Emotion and adaptation.* New York: Oxford University Press.

Lehrer, J. (2009). *How we decide.* Boston: Houghton Mifflin Harcourt.

Levy, K., and Kelly, K. (2010). Sex differences in jealousy: A contribution from attachment theory. *Psychological Science, 21*(2), 168–73.

Loue, S. (2006). *Sexual partnering, sexual practices, and health.* New York: Springer.

Lupton, D. (1998). *The emotional self: A sociocultural exploration.* Thousand Oaks, CA: Sage.

McLuhan, M., and McLuhan, E. (1988). *Laws of media: The new science.* Toronto: University of Toronto Press.

Mead, M. (1968). Jealousy: Primitive and civilized. In F. Lindenfeld (Ed.), *Radical perspectives on social problems* (pp. 92–103). New York: Macmillan.

Mint, P. (2007a). Polyamory and feminism. http://freaksexual.wordpress.com/2007/03/27/polyamory-and-feminism/

Mint, P. (2007b). The Strange Credibility of Polyamory. http://freaksexual.wordpress.com/2007/11/27/the-strange-credibility-of-polyamory/

Mint, P. (2008). Poly is not about sex, except when it is. http://freaksexual.wordpress.com/2008/01/31/polyamory-is-not-about-the-sex-except-when-it-is/

Munson, M., and Stelboum, J.P. (1999). *The lesbian polyamory reader: Open relationships, non-monogamy, and casual sex.* New York: Routledge.

Ngai, S. (2005). *Ugly feelings.* Cambridge, MA: Harvard University Press.

Noël, M.J. (2006). Progressive polyamory: Considering issues of diversity. *Sexualities, 9*(5), 602–20.

Overall, C. (1998). Monogamy, nonmonogamy and identity. *Hypatia: A Journal of Feminist Philosophy, 13*(4), 1–17.

Parkinson, B., Fischer, A., and Manstead, A. (2005). *Emotions in social relations: Cultural, group and interpersonal processes.* New York: Psychology Press.

Parrott, W. (1991). The emotional experiences of envy and jealousy. In P. Salovey (Ed.), *The psychology of jealousy and envy* (pp. 3–30). New York: Guilford Press.

Petersen, A. (2004). *Engendering emotions.* New York: Palgrave Macmillan.

Plummer, K. (2001). *Documents of life 2: An invitation to critical humanism.* London: Sage.

Rambukkana, N. (2004). Uncomfortable bridges: The bisexual politics of outing polyamory. *Journal of Bisexuality, 4*(3–4), 141–54.

Rambukkana, N. (2010). Sex, space and discourse: Non/monogamy and intimate privilege in the public sphere. In M. Barker and D. Langdridge (Eds.), *Understanding non-monogamies* (pp. 237–42). New York: Routledge.

Ravenscroft, A. (2004). *Polyamory: Roadmaps for the clueless and hopeful.* Santa Fe: Fenris Brothers.

Reddy, W. (1999). Emotional liberty: Politics and history in the anthropology of emotions. *Cultural Anthropology, 14*(2), 256–88.

Ritchie, A., and Barker, M. (2006). "There aren't words for what we do or how we feel so we have to make them up": Constructing polyamorous language in a culture of compulsory monogamy. *Sexualities, 9*(5), 584–601.

Robinson, M. (2013). Polyamory and monogamy as strategic identities. *Journal of Bisexuality, 13*(1), 21–38.

Robinson, V. (1997). My baby just cares for me: Feminism, heterosexuality and non-monogamy. *Journal of Gender Studies, 6*(2), 143–57.

Rosenberg, M. (2003). *Non-violent communication: A language of life.* Encinitas, CA: Puddledancer Press.

Rubin, G. (1993). Thinking sex: Notes for a radical theory of the politics of sexuality. In H. Abelone, M.A. Barale, and D. Halperin (Eds.), *The lesbian and gay studies reader* (pp. 3–44). New York: Routledge.

Ryan, C., and Jetha, C. (2010). *Sex at dawn: The prehistoric origins of modern sexuality.* New York: HarperCollins.

Salovey, P. (1991). *The psychology of jealousy and envy.* New York: Guilford Press.

Schwartz, B. (2004). *The paradox of choice: Why more is less.* New York: Ecco.

Sheff, E. (2005). Polyamorous women, sexual subjectivity and power. *Journal of Contemporary Ethnography, 34*(3), 251–83.

Sheff, E. (2006). Poly-hegemonic masculinities. *Sexualities, 9*(5), 621–42.

Sheff, E. (2010). Strategies in polyamorous parenting. In M. Barker and D. Langdridge (Eds.), *Understanding non-monogamies* (pp. 169–81). New York: Routledge.

Sheff, E. (2013). *The polyamorists next door: Inside multiple-partner relationships and families.* Lanham, MD: Rowman & Littlefield Publishers.

Sheff, E., and Hammers, C. (2011). The privilege of perversities: Race, class and education among polyamorists and kinksters. *Psychology and Sexuality, 2*(3), 198–233.

Siegel, D. (2010). *Mindsight: The new science of personal transformation.* New York: Bantam Books.

Simmel, G. (1955). *Conflict and web of affiliations*. New York: Free Press.

Speed, A., and Ganstead, S.W. (1997). Romantic popularity and mate preferences: A peer nomination study. *Personality and Social Psychology Bulletin*, 23(9), 928–36.

Staudenmaier, P. (2001). Slipping the ties that bind: Varietism, compulsory monogamy and loving more. http://www.polyamoryonline.org/articles/slipping.html

Stearns, P. (1989). *Jealousy: The evolution of an emotion in American history*. New York: New York University Press.

Sue, D., Capodilupo, C., Torino, G., Bucceri, J., Holder, A., Nadal, K., and Esquilin, M. (2007). Racial microaggressions in everyday life: Implications for clinical practice. *American Psychologist*, 62(4), 271–86.

Tanenbaum, L. (2000). *Slut! Growing up female with a bad reputation*. New York: Harper.

Taormino, T. (2008). *Opening Up: A guide to creating and sustaining open relationships*. Berkeley, CA: Cleis Press.

Tauchert, A. (2002). Fuzzy gender: Between female-embodiment and intersex. *Journal of Gender Studies*, 11(1), 29–38.

Thoits, P. (2012). Emotional deviance and mental disorder. In D. Spencer, K. Walby, and A. Hunt (Eds.), *Emotions matter: A relational approach to emotions* (pp. 201–22). Toronto: University of Toronto Press.

Turner, J., and Stets, J. (2005). *The sociology of emotions*. Cambridge: Cambridge University Press.

Uslaner, E. (2001). Producing and consuming trust. *Political Science Quarterly*, 115(4), 569–90.

Vance, C. (1989). *Pleasure and danger: Exploring female sexuality*. London: Pandora Press.

Veaux, F. (2006). Practical jealousy management. http://www.morethantwo.com/practicaljealousy.pdf.

Weeks, J. (1985). *Sexuality and its discontents: Meanings, myths and modern sexualities*. London and New York: Routledge.

Weeks, J. (2003). *Sexuality*. 2nd ed. London: Routledge.

Weeks, J. (2008). Traps we set ourselves. *Sexualities*, 11(1–2), 27–33.

Weeks, J., Heaphy, B., and Donovan, C. (2001). *Same-sex intimacies*. London: Routledge.

Weitzman, G. (1999). What psychology professionals should know about polyamory. http://www.polyamory.org/~joe/polypaper.htm

West, C. (1996). *Lesbian polyfidelity*. San Francisco and Montreal: Booklegger Publishing.

White, G., and Mullen, P. (1989). *Jealousy: Theory, research and clinical strategies*. New York: Guilford Press.

Wilkins, A.C. (2004). So full of myself as a chick: Goth women, sexual independence, and gender egalitarianism. *Gender & Society, 18*(3), 328–49.

Williams, S., and Bendelow, G. (1996). The "emotional" body. *Body & Society, 2*(3), 125–39.

Wolfe, L. (2008). On kittens and the very invented culture of polyamory. *Electronic Journal of Sexuality Studies, 11.*

Wolfe, N. (1992). *The beauty myth: How images of beauty are used against women.* New York: HarperCollins.

Wosick-Correa, K. (2010). Agreements, rules, and agentic fidelity in polyamorous relationships. *Psychology & Sexuality, 1*(1), 44–61.

Wosick-Correa, K. (2008). Contemporary fidelities: Sex, love and commitment in romantic relationships. *Dissertation Abstracts International: Humanities and Social Sciences, 68*(09), 4080.

Yates, C. (2007). *Masculine jealousy and contemporary cinema.* London: Palgrave Macmillan.

Yates, C. (2000). Masculinity and good enough jealousy. *Psychoanalytic Studies, 2*(1), 77–88.

Zell, M.G. ([1990] 2014). Bouquet of lovers. *Green Egg Magazine,* 163 (June 2014), 9–12.

Zembylas, M., and Fendler, L. (2007). Reframing emotion in education through lenses of parrhesia and care of the self. *Studies in Philosophy and Education, 6*(4), 319–33.

Index